WAITING

STUDIES IN SOCIAL INEQUALITY

This book series is devoted to examining poverty and inequality in its many forms, including the takeoff in economic inequality, increasing spatial segregation, and ongoing changes in gender, racial, and ethnic inequality.

WAITING

ON

RETIREMENT

Aging and Economic Insecurity
in Low-Wage Work

MARY GATTA

STANFORD UNIVERSITY PRESS
Stanford, California

Stanford University Press

Stanford, California

©2019 by the Board of Trustees of the Leland Stanford Junior University. All rights reserved.

Printed in the United States of America on acid-free, archival-quality paper

Library of Congress Cataloging-in-Publication Data

Names: Gatta, Mary Lizabeth, 1972– author.
Title: Waiting on retirement : aging and economic insecurity in low-wage work / Mary Gatta.
Description: Stanford, California : Stanford University Press, 2018. | Series: Studies in social inequality | Includes bibliographical references and index.
Identifiers: LCCN 2018009498 (print) | LCCN 2018015963 (ebook) | ISBN 9781503607415 (e-book) | ISBN 9780804799959 (cloth : alk. paper) | ISBN 9781503607408 (pbk. : alk. paper) | ISBN 9781503607415 (ebook)
Subjects: LCSH: Retirement—Economic aspects—United States. | Working poor—Retirement—United States. | Restaurants—Employees—Retirement—United States. | Restaurants—United States—Employees—Economic conditions.
Classification: LCC HQ1063.2.U6 (ebook) | LCC HQ1063.2.U6 G38 2018 (print) | DDC 306.3/80973—dc23
LC record available at https://lccn.loc.gov/2018009498

Typeset by Newgen in Adobe Garamond 10.5/15

Cover design: George Kirkpatrick

Cover photo: iStockphoto

This book is dedicated to the memory of Anthony Bourdain.
By sharing meals around the globe, Anthony not only
introduced us to the beauty in diverse cultures and communities;
he also served as a tireless advocate for the many workers who
cook our meals, mix our drinks, serve our dinners,
and wash our dishes in restaurants throughout the world.

May those workers—and indeed all working
families—live in a world where economic security
and retirement are not elusive dreams.

Contents

Acknowledgments

A book is a journey that one does not take alone, and this book is no exception. This final product has been years in the making and truly took a village to come to life.

I am greatly indebted to my former colleagues at Wider Opportunities for Women (WOW) in Washington, D.C. Not only did they provide the intellectual space to allow me to explore the issues of aging and work; they were among the most dedicated and passionate co-workers I had the good fortune to work alongside. I am forever appreciative for my time at WOW and in awe of the fifty years of advocacy and research for women and their families that the organization provided to our community. I greatly miss WOW but continue to be inspired as I watch the organization's work influence policy and programs.

I am also grateful for the support and insights from my faculty colleagues throughout the Rutgers University and City University of New York (CUNY) systems who have consistently been supportive and encouraging over the years. Several colleagues in my network went above and beyond to help shape this work. Deborah Harris at Texas State University provided critical contacts and feedback that improved the book. Teófilo Reyes at Restaurant Opportunities Center United (ROC United) provided an invaluable network of potential interviewers and was an early advocate for this book. Special mention must be made of Luisa Deprez at the University of Southern Maine. Luisa spent countless hours providing constructive, in-depth, and thoughtful feedback that made the book much stronger than I ever could have alone. Finally,

I am thankful for the anonymous peer reviewers who took the time to help shape this book.

I have been fortunate to work with an amazing editorial team at Stanford University. Margo Fleming saw the value in this work very early, was open to countless conversations, and shepherded this work through countless drafts. Marcela Maxfield helped shape this work into its final product, providing thoughtful feedback and stepping into the project without missing a beat. And Olivia Bartz provided critical support throughout the process.

Several parts of this research were supported by grants. The Henry and Marylin Taub Foundation provided grant support for the focus groups in New Jersey, and Atlantic Philanthropies provided funding to WOW that allowed for the focus groups in Massachusetts. In addition, I was awarded a City University of New York (CUNY) Book Completion grant to help finish the final year of writing.

I am also thankful to my husband, Mike Glory, who has helped to inform my research on restaurant and service workers for decades. He spent his career in the hospitality industry and, fortunately, working for good employers; his insights and experience help to show us a path forward that continues to improve a job that so many love.

Finally, I am indebted to the workers and retirees who gave their time to meet with me to share their stories and lives. The book could not exist without them, and I firmly believe that their voices must be central to any discussions—be it in Washington, D.C., or in any state capital—if we truly want to ensure that all Americans can age with economic security.

Prologue

The crisis that aging workers face as they attempt to march to retirement crosses many occupational and class lines. Americans overall report anxiety about their financial security in retirement. Those who have some savings and investments worry about whether they have enough put away or if the funds will be wiped out in the marketplace. Those who own a home hope that their asset will have a decent economic value when they retire. And so many are concerned that one health crisis will leave them not only sick but economically broken. These worries are significant, but far too many workers have even more dire fears. Many Americans lack any resources—savings, homeownership, or investments—as they age and face an even more uncertain future. Workers who have spent their years in low-wage jobs are among the most vulnerable population. What we can learn from their experience aging in the workforce can provide critical insights into the retirement prospects for them and all of us. This book is my attempt to bring aging low-wage workers' experiences to light to make clear the reality of retirement when workers do not earn enough to get by.

When I picked up my first tray of hamburgers and fries to serve to a table of hungry customers, I was a student in my early twenties earning money to help cover the costs of my education. I worked alongside an eclectic group of waiters and waitresses, including fellow students who were trying to defray college costs; twenty-somethings who were using restaurant work to earn a side income until their careers in teaching, health care, or financial services took off; and mothers providing a second income to support their families. There was also a group who called themselves "lifers." The "lifers" were workers, often over 40 years old, who had spent their careers in restaurant work and were not planning on leaving. This group in particular was dependent on a subminimum wage—we were earning $2.13 an hour—and the generosity of customers' tips to cover their monthly rent, food, and expenses for the duration of their working years. We all shared frustrations when customers stiffed us—leaving us with no tip for our service at their table. And, almost every time, this tip loss was framed in terms of their own economic struggles—a lost meal for their children or difficulty in making rent that month. Although we received biweekly paychecks, each paycheck would almost always be a VOID check, meaning that once taxes were taken out of our low hourly pay, there was no income left for us. I vividly remember some of my co-workers just laughing at their VOID check each pay period, and then tearing it up to throw in the trash.

While the lifers I worked with often shared the economic, emotional, and educational struggles they experienced daily, there were questions that I never asked them all those years ago—"What is going to happen when you can no longer work?" or "Are you planning for retirement?" During slow times in the restaurant we would talk about how hard it was to make rent but never how hard it was to save for a postwork future. Perhaps it was emotionally easier to stay in the present, or maybe my co-workers didn't imagine that there would be a time when they could not work. It is their unspoken questions that motivate this book. What are the experiences of low-wage workers as they march toward retirement? How are workers who are barely getting by preparing for a time when they can no longer work? Are they forging new paths to a possibly secure retirement, or is the reality of their working lives making any semblance of retirement elusive?

To answer these questions, I spent time with restaurant workers to gain a more complete picture of the lives of low-wage workers and their growing concerns for their futures. To put this in the starkest terms, when I asked a twenty-year bartending veteran how he was planning for his future, he replied, "I have no savings, no retirement plan. I am just going to keep on working and hope I drop dead behind the bar." His response brings to the forefront so many questions about our growing numbers of low-wage laborers. What happens when you spend your life working in a job that barely offers the income to survive? Naturally, you will find that your financial struggles are even more difficult if and when you retire. How can they be expected to save for a retirement when they cannot pay for basic expenses—such as housing, health care, and groceries? What's more, low wages in one's working years lead to even lower social security payments in retirement. This means that people who are already living on very little will be living on even less. Sadly there is a good chance that this will be the reality for close to half of Americans who are working today and merely scraping by. Looking at restaurant work—which has not provided stable retirement paths for many of its workers—provides us insights into how low-wage workers in a variety of industries are attempting to survive when they can no longer work. Could it be that, as the bartender told me, hoping for a quick death while one is still able to work is actually the only viable retirement option?

Why Restaurant Work?

As with so many ethnographers, my interest in low-wage work grew out of my own experiences working in the low-wage job of waiting tables. It seemed fitting to return to restaurant work for this book. Delving into an investigation of restaurant workers, we can learn a great deal about the improbability of retirement in jobs that pay too little. Throughout this book it will become clear that restaurant work, for the most part, is representative of low-wage work that cannot provide a stable route to any semblance of retirement—the wages are low, the benefits are almost nonexistent, and there is little opportunity for real advancement to economic security. Moreover, our service economy (restaurant work, retail, home health aides) is projected to continue to grow, so larger numbers of workers will find themselves working their entire lives without a real possibility of retirement. And, as I demonstrate with existing data, it is not just low-wage workers who are facing retirement challenges. Instead, a considerable number of younger workers outside restaurant work (Generation Xers and younger baby boomers) are approaching retirement with little or no savings. By focusing on the lived experiences of restaurant workers at different points in their lives, I can highlight a larger point that extends beyond restaurant workers—the impossibility of retirement in jobs that pay too little and lack the savings vehicles and benefits to prepare for long-term economic security. Further, while restaurant work provides us insight into the challenges of retiring in low-wage work, 20 percent of restaurant jobs are "good jobs"—ones that offer the wages and benefits for a more secure future.[1] Therefore, the practices found in this smaller share of restaurant work provide insights in how to improve low-wage work so that workers can age with economic security. In sum, restaurant work provides insight to both the impossibility of retirement in jobs that don't pay enough and ways to improve the prospects of economic security.

How is restaurant work representative of many low-wage jobs in the U.S. labor market? First, the demographic composite of the restaurant workforce is representative of the low-wage labor market as a whole in the United States. Second, the bulk (80 percent) of restaurant jobs are not good jobs in terms of labor market rewards: workers are paid minimum and subminimum wages,[2] lack schedule control (making work/family balance and opportunities to gain additional income difficult), and often come without health care and retirement savings benefits. These job characteristics are found in many other low-wage work environments. Retail workers, for instance, are paid minimum wages with few benefits and often lack predictable schedules—leaving them uncertain of their income on a weekly basis. Third, restaurant work (like other low-wage work) is growing. For instance, similar to home health aides, restaurant workers are not susceptible to offshoring, as one needs their cook or bartender in the same place that they are eating. Restaurant work also provides insight into some of the most grievous instances of workplace practices, particularly working for tipped wages and occupational health and safety risks. These structural similarities and distinctions allow restaurant work to be an important case study, providing numerous insights and understandings much broader than the case itself.

Let's first turn to the demographic composition of restaurant workers, particularly how they are representative of the larger low-wage labor market. Perhaps surprising to some, restaurant workers are not made up of all young people saving for college, like I was. They are workers of all ages—from students to parents—and many stay in the industry for twenty to forty years.[3] Economist Heidi Shierholz has noted that occupations in the restaurant industry are also highly gendered and racialized, and this stratification contributes to disparities in labor market rewards. As compared to men, women are more likely to work in the lowest-paid tiers of cashiers/counter attendants, hosts, and wait staff. And African American and Hispanic workers are also disproportionately employed in low-paid restaurant occupations (such as dishwashers, dining room attendants, and cashiers) as compared to white workers. In contrast, white non-Hispanic workers are more likely to be in the higher-paying occupations of hosts/hostesses, wait staff, bartenders, and managers.[4] Race and gender both play a significant role in whether a worker is among the 20 percent of restaurant workers who have the opportunity for livable wages during their tenure and the possibility for a more secure retirement.

Not only does the demographic composite of restaurant work mirror the larger low-wage labor market, but so do many of the work structures and employment conditions that shape economic opportunities for their workers in ways that often hinder economic security as they consider any form of retirement. First, most restaurant workers receive low pay, in some cases the lowest pay in the labor market. The median hourly wage, including tips, is $10.00 an hour, compared to $18.00 an hour outside the industry. Shierholz refers to this as the wage penalty of restaurant work. She notes that even accounting for demographic differences between restaurant workers and other workers, restaurant workers have hourly wages that are 17 percent lower than those of similar workers outside the industry. The largest restaurant industry occupation is waiter/waitress—making up nearly a quarter of all the jobs at an average wage (including tips) of $10.15 per hour. Within the restaurant industry, the lowest-paid occupation is cashiers/counter attendants, earning

$8.23 per hour, and the highest-paid workers are managers, earning on average $15.42 per hour.[5] This latter point brings into question whether there is any real upward mobility in lower-wage work. For example, one would consider a promotion to a management position a route to economic security, but with the median income hovering around $15 per hour, even higher-paid restaurant jobs do not secure a living wage in many parts of the United States. Shierholz found that one in six restaurant workers live blow the official poverty line, and more than two in five workers (43 percent) live with less than half the income that would qualify them as reaching the poverty line.[6] Further, ROC United researchers found that restaurant workers hold seven of the ten lowest-paying occupations in the United States—earning less than farm workers and domestic workers.[7]

In 2014, while working at Wider Opportunities for Women, I partnered with ROC United to survey restaurant workers on the Jersey Shore after Hurricane Sandy made a direct hit on the state. Eighty-seven percent of the workers we surveyed worked for tips. Of those, 82 percent earned less than the state minimum wage of $7.25 per hour in 2013. And once state and federal taxes are applied to their pay, their paychecks are voided out, signifying that their wages did not equal owed taxes. They then would owe back taxes at the end of the year. While living on tips can be a route to economic security for some, for most workers it is economically precarious. Workers' tips, and hence their economic security, depend on customers' whims. Research finds that tips are only weakly related to a worker's attentiveness, effort, or skills but more likely dependent on the server's gender, race, and attractiveness, or smaller gestures disconnected from the work of serving meals.[8] This aesthetic labor is common in other low-wage industries such as retail jobs—and as workers age, they tend to have less and less of the aesthetics needed to secure jobs.[9] And in more expensive restaurants, where larger tips are more prevalent, women and people of color are less likely to find work.

However, financial insecurity is not just a product of a subminimum wage and minimal tips. Restaurant workers, like other low-wage workers, may also be the victim of wage theft—the deliberate withholding of wages to which workers are legally entitled—which comes in many forms, among them not paying workers for preparing their work stations for their shifts, not paying overtime wages, charging workers a percentage of their tips when customers use credit cards, and other illegal workplace practices. In my research with ROC United on New Jersey restaurant workers, 70 percent of surveyed workers reported that they did not receive overtime pay when they worked more than forty hours a week, eight hours per day, or six days per week. Forty percent reported that they had worked off the clock without being paid their hourly wage in the past year.[10] And while wage theft negatively affects all workers, those earning $2.13 an hour are particularly vulnerable.

To earn the wages needed to support their families, workers must work the hours and days that restaurants are busiest, which tend to be evenings, weekends, and holidays. Working these nontraditional hours creates significant challenges in balancing work and family issues, caring for family members, and, if needed, arranging for child care. And it makes it quite difficult to secure a second job to make ends meet. As a result, workers' low wages are compounded by a high degree of schedule inflexibility, making their economic insecurity even more precarious, much of which is tied to the common practice of "volatile workplace scheduling." Here, both the number of hours and the timing of those hours can change day to day, week to week, and season to season at the discretion of management. This unpredictability means that a worker may have to work different hours and different days each week with no consistent days off. Further, schedules are often posted with little advance notice (often only a day or two), making it very difficult to schedule life appointments around work.

Additionally, managers can make last-minute changes to the work schedule once it is posted if it appears that customer traffic may be higher or lower than anticipated. Managers may also send a worker home if the establishment is not busy. And if the restaurant is busy, workers who are scheduled for an end time may be forced to stay later, a practice known as mandatory overtime. Under the Fair Labor Standards

Act, workers have virtually no legal recourse to challenge terminations or retaliations for refusing mandatory overtime. These last-minute requirements and unpredictable schedules create challenges for workers, especially those who depend on public transportation to get to and from work and those who have family obligations. In addition, workers are sometimes "on call," scheduled to work only if the shift is busy. These workers need to be able to leave at a moment's notice to go to work. Further, schedules are affected by the time of the year: tourism and holiday seasons can lead to longer hours for workers. All this makes estimating one's income a challenge. And if one does not know what they will be earning annually, it is hard to judge how much, if anything they can save.

Low-wage work has not just a negative economic impact on workers; it also has a physical impact. Much analysis of service economy jobs focuses on its interactive elements, often ignoring or overlooking the physical dimensions of such work. Yet as Karla Erickson notes in her study of restaurants, the "skillful use of the body is necessary for this work: a staff that communicates well will get so accustomed to passing each other, switching places, transferring trays, sharing space and helping each other that words no longer are necessary during the busiest part of the evening."[11] As a result, workers' bodies become part of the work they perform. This is important as their bodies age in the workplace. The long hours and low wages contribute to the heavy toll that waiting tables puts on workers' bodies. Servers carry heavy, hot plates quickly through the dining room, sometimes balancing up to six or seven plates at a time. As floors in kitchens are often slippery and backstage service spaces tend to be quite crowded, servers need considerable agility to maneuver. Quite astutely, Erickson comments, "You need to be in good shape to wait tables, but you don't get in shape doing it."[12]

The degree of physical work is further compounded as workers report that they do not often get formal breaks in their workday and can work ten to twelve hours without once sitting down. In my ethnographic work at the Café Red restaurant years ago, managers told me that they provide servers with a "choice" regarding breaks, but many times servers would rather continue taking tables than take a break (as taking a break means forfeiting at least one round of tips).[13] Yet my field observation showed something different: during busy times managers would inform servers that they would try to give breaks, but if the restaurant remained busy the servers would have to work through their break. Breaks therefore became a privilege. In lieu of formal breaks, servers had to squeeze in time between serving customers to go to the bathroom and eat meals. Often they would get food and then place it somewhere in the kitchen where it might sit for hours, with the server nibbling at bites whenever they found a free second.

Such a lifestyle, when maintained long enough, puts strains on muscles, bones, and digestive systems. On-the-job injuries can affect long-term health. ROC United director Saru Jayaraman notes that the U.S. Department of Labor ranked the restaurant industry as the third highest in total number in nonfatal occupational injuries and illness. Nearly 200,000 accidents are reported in restaurants each year, and ROC United members reported that almost half (49 percent) of those workers had suffered work-related cuts and 46 percent had been burned on the job. One study found that hot grease in fast-food restaurants accounted for half of the burn injuries and for more than 40 percent of the burns in full-service cafés.[14] Workers also often report backaches and sore muscles from carrying heavy trays and being on their feet for long periods of time.

And the experiences of restaurant workers are similar to those of other low-wage workers.[15] Liz Borkowski and Celeste Monforton estimate that the number of work-related fatalities, illnesses, and injuries experienced by workers in low-wage jobs exceeds 1.72 million.[16] For instance, home health aides must lift heavy bodies and the Occupational Safety and Health Administration (OSHA) reports that the most common injuries reported included sprains, strains, and musculoskeletal injuries, which can haunt workers for years.[17] Similarly, a 2010 study found that retail workers experience lasting impacts of musculoskeletal disorders and carpal tunnel syndrome.[18]

The restaurant environment itself, like other service workplaces, also matters for workers' long-term health risks. Secondhand smoke can cause or aggravate many respiratory problems, including bronchitis and asthma, and increase the risk of heart attack and some types of cancers. Excessive and constant noise (such as loud music) is one of the primary causes of job stress and fatigue. For instance, a study of urban music club employees, including waiters, waitresses, and bartenders, found that the clubs' noise levels far exceeded the maximum exposure limit allowed by the government, according to the National Institute for Occupational Safety and Health (NIOSH). The authors concluded that the employees were at significant risk of hearing loss later in life.[19]

Further, the nature of shift work itself causes both short-term and long-term problems for workers, such as shift work sleep disorder (SWSD), which, according to the Cleveland Clinic, is a sleep disorder that affects people who frequently rotate shifts or work at night. The schedules of these workers go against the body's natural circadian rhythm, and individuals have difficulty adjusting to the different sleep and wake schedule. SWSD, as defined by the Cleveland Clinic, consists of a constant or recurrent pattern of sleep interruption that results in difficulty sleeping or excessive sleepiness. This disorder is common in people who work nontraditional hours, usually between ten p.m. and six a.m. In fact, while Americans are increasingly getting less sleep each night, those who earn the least are far more likely to get less than seven hours of sleep a night. A 2014 Gallup Poll found that about half of people in households earning less than $23,000 annually sleep less than six hours a night, as compared to only one third of individuals in households earning over $75,000.[20] The American Sleep Association noted that shift work sleeping disorders may have devastating long-term effects as well. Employees working in shift work positions for more than ten years have shown drastically increased rates of heart disease and gastrointestinal disease, up to a 300 percent increase in the incidence rates of the diseases compared to the general population.[21] In a rather disturbing study, neuroscientists had mice imitate the schedules of shift workers; the rodents' brain cells began permanently dying off after only days of keeping that schedule.[22]

Despite all the economic and physical demands, many of these workers rarely receive fringe benefits that could help defray life expenses. Only 14 percent of workers receive health insurance from their employer, compared with roughly half of other workers. And only 8.4 percent of restaurant workers are included in a retirement plan at their job—one fifth the rate of pension coverage outside the restaurant industry.[23] So the workers who are experiencing significant health impacts from their work often lack the health and economic resources to address the problems.

There is one final reason why restaurant work provides an important snapshot into the low-wage labor market. While most restaurant jobs are not good jobs in terms of labor market rewards, a small number are good jobs. ROC United research shows that 20 percent of the jobs in the industry provide livable wages. These are largely chef, server, and bartender positions in fine-dining restaurants.[24] Yet perhaps not surprisingly, they are predominantly held by white men. However, these jobs do represent what we would consider "good jobs"—economic-security wages, health care and retirement benefits, and sometimes union protections. This means that there are models in the restaurant workplaces, along with workers' case studies, that can be drawn upon to present a way forward in the low-wage labor market that can offer more economic security for workers as they march to retirement.

In this book we meet low-wage workers as they struggle to get by and plan ahead for a life without work. Their stories are meant to demonstrate the gravity of their situation but also highlight what challenges lie ahead for all of us. Throughout this journey we look to restaurant work as a classic example of unstable, low-wage work that—for a significant portion of workers—provided neither the income or the kinds of benefits that could lead to a stable retirement. There are many other kinds of low-wage work like this in American industries. Employment in the service economy is growing as a share of the overall economy, which has devastating implications for retirement for more and more of the workforce. I use the example of restaurant work to make the larger point about the impossibility of retiring when jobs pay too little to make ends meet (let alone save), have no health or retirement benefits, and offer few options for real advancement.

Sadly, the retirement crisis is already upon us and will only get worse for everyone as baby boomers retire. Consequences will be felt most acutely by low-wage workers, as in the case of restaurant workers, many of whom are already struggling to make ends meet while they work. If middle-class retirees are struggling and low-wage workers are struggling, we can assume this problem transcends boundaries of socioeconomic class and will only get worse for everyone unless drastic policy changes are made. If we begin to see all our experiences as intimately connected, we can then develop and implement collective policy responses that will improve economic security for all.

WAITING ON RETIREMENT

CHAPTER 1

The New Normal

The United States is facing an imminent grim reality: more and more American workers are not able to retire. They are often too young to die but too poor not to work. By focusing on the experiences of low-wage workers as they are stare down the retirement pike as well as current retirees as they try to maintain economic security, this book investigates the potentially catastrophic nature of that reality. The analysis is framed not only in terms of what their lived experiences mean for their own economic security but also what this suggests about the economic future for all of us. So much of our national dialogue is focused on how economic insecurity impacts working families' daily experiences and not how it impacts their ability to save. Many people cringe as they hear horrific stories of working Americans having to decide between food and medicine, accruing massive credit card debt, working multiple shifts without any control over their schedule, going to work sick because they will be fired if they don't come in, commuting on several bus lines for hours to get to their minimum-wage job because they can't afford a car, and losing their homes to live among the growing population of the employed homeless. These scenarios indicate a serious economic and moral crisis, but Americans are not prepared for the crisis to come when these individuals are no longer employed.

The unfortunate reality is that we do not have to wait thirty years to get a glimpse of this upcoming crisis. Today many Americans are living without the savings needed to be secure during their working years and beyond. Many of these workers have spent their lives in traditionally low-wage work and did not have enough income to save. Increasingly, middle-wage workers find themselves in a similar economic situation. In 2016, the Federal Reserve found that 47 percent of Americans could not cover an emergency expense of $400.[1] While this savings gap is distressing, the lack of a savings reserve becomes even more significant as one ages. In 2015, Wider Opportunities for Women (WOW)[2] found that more than 50 percent of elderly individuals and couples lacked basic economic security in their retirement. Although these folks worked for years—many of which spanned booming economic times—along with having retirement savings of some sort, their economic reality is far from rosy. And while the situation for current retirees is alarming, the picture is even worse for those who are approaching retirement age. In 2015, a stunning 35 million Americans—26 percent of our workforce—earned less than $10.55 an hour[3] toiling in the growing low-wage jobs offered by our nation's hospitality centers, retail stores, and child care and health care systems. Not only do these positions pay little, they tend to not offer retirement savings plans or health care benefits.

What could the future look like? Economist Teresa Ghilarducci grimly predicts that by 2050 there could be 25 million poor elderly Americans. Her back-of-the-envelope estimate is based on the Organisation for Economic Co-operation and Development (OECD) measure of impoverishment and the aging baby boomer population. To put her estimate in perspective, in 2010 an alarming 8.9 million elderly Americans were living in poverty. According to Ghilarducci's estimate, elder poverty will increase by 180 percent over the next forty years. If the projections bear out by midcentury, the number of American seniors living in poverty will be at unprecedented levels. Ghilarducci suggests that a portion of the increase is related to the aging boomer population—by 2050 the elderly population will have increased by 106 percent[4]—however, that doesn't account for all of the increase. Instead, the surge in poverty is not just about the increased number of older Americans; it is much more tied to the weak retirement system and labor market inequities in the United States.

So many Americans are depending on social security as their main, and often only, source of guaranteed income in retirement—yet many have anxieties that even that income will not be available to them at the level they would need. Joseph Coleman, summarizing the trends in American retirement patterns, highlights the ever-concerning notion that social security is estimated to be able to pay workers full benefits only for the next two decades, unless a major reform is implemented. After that, payouts are expected to drop to 75 percent as the trust fund runs dry.[5] Social security, however, is just part of the picture. The increased number of workers with defined contribution plans and the corresponding decrease in the number of workers with defined benefit pension plans contributes to the economic insecurity we are facing. He finds that in 1975, close to 60 percent of private-sector workers had defined benefit pensions—which translated into guaranteed benefits upon retirement. Today, many Americas rely on 401(k)-type accounts to supplement their social security income. This shift from traditional pensions has increased economic insecurity and widened retirement gaps across race, ethnicity, gender, marital status, and education. Yet not only have defined benefit plans shifted to defined contribution plans, but the risk in saving for one's retirement has been transferred to the individual.[6] Of course, this shift to individual risk is not just part of our retirement system; the same is true for education and health care, along with other aspects of our lives.

But this was not always the case. In 1933 the passage of President Franklin Roosevelt's New Deal created the Social Security Act and the Wagner-Peyser Act, both of which ensured that workers had access to old-age insurance and unemployment insurance. The programs were expanded and enhanced under President Lyndon Johnson's Great Society agenda in 1964. Through social insurance programs including disability insurance, Medicare, and Medicaid, workers were protected from many macroeconomic changes. In addition, many workers had secure jobs, good wages, health and disability insurance, and pension benefits. Indeed, the goals of many initiatives from the New Deal to the Great Society and beyond have been to make work "pay"—to assist individuals by providing skill training, educational opportunities, wage protections, and opportunities to collectively bargain and enable them to provide themselves and/or their families with the security necessary for day-to-day living. What this translates to is improving workforce preparedness of low-skilled workers, enabling low-wage workforce avenues of mobility (the ability to move up, retain jobs, and be promoted), practices that demonstrate care for workers and preempt worker difficulties, and access to higher education and vocational training. In addition, social insurance programs such as social security, disability, and health care help provide income and support when a worker can no longer work. These programs, along with an expanding economy, helped a generation of Americans attain economic security.

However, the New Deal social gains have been progressively chipped away over the decades. Union membership, once a route to security, has steadily declined largely because the legal and political environment prevents private-sector workers from freely exercising their right to join a union. As a result, in 2015 only 11 percent of the American workforce was unionized,[7] meaning fewer workers have access to collectively bargained benefits including retirement and health care. The economic results are dire. In 2016, Economic Policy Institute (EPI) researchers found that the effect of union decline on nonunion wages translates into millions of lost dollars for American workers and their families. In 2013 approximately 40.2 million private-sector men and 32.9 million private-sector women were working full-time, were not senior managers, and did not belong to a union. To put this into monetary terms, the union decline has contributed to a total decline in weekly income of $2.1 billion for non-union workers.[8]

Coupled with the decline of unions, Americans have increasingly been asked to prepare for and plan for their retirement themselves, while dealing with a decreased social safety net during their work lives. This neoliberal political ideology views dependency as a negative attribute and, as Marianne Cooper states, "celebrates risk and uncertainty as self-reliance."[9] The New Deal social contract—which had as its cornerstone that individuals had clear social rights—was replaced with a free-market approach that minimizes the role of government in individuals' lives. Through this policy shift, individuals found themselves moving away from defined benefit to defined contribution plans. Employers no longer had long-term liabilities, and workers had to make their own choices regarding how much and how to save for their futures within the free market. And individuals had to then live with the results of these choices—whether they were good or bad—and the gambles have not turned out great for many workers. As Coleman notes: "Employees preoccupied with paying today's bills have not focused on distant retirement; enrollment is lacking; participants don't put enough money into the accounts and they don't invest as wisely as pension-account managers. And then, of course, something like the Great Recession can come along and wipe out investments just as participants are about to embark on retirement."[10]

But even as precarious as defined contribution plans can be, many Americans still don't even have a plan. A 2015 Government Accounting Office (GAO) report found that nearly 29 percent of American households with members who are age 55 or older have neither retirement savings nor traditional pension plans, regardless of whether they spent their careers in low-wage or middle-wage jobs. And for those nearing retirement who do have some savings, it is woefully inadequate. The median amount of savings for all households with individuals who are 55 to 64 years old is $104,000 and just $148,000 for households with members who are 65 to 74 years old. According to the report this translates to roughly a projected annuity of $310 or $649 a month, respectively—nowhere near enough to survive anywhere in the United States. And among all working households, almost half (45.3 percent) have no retirement savings accounts. This reality is quite jarring when we look across age groups, particularly those close to traditional retirement age. Forty-five percent of workers who are 35 to 44 years old have no retirement savings; this is also the case for 43 percent of workers who are 45 to 54 years old and 40 percent of those who are 56 to 64 years old.[11] Without a safety net or personal savings, many hardworking Americans will find themselves struggling even more as they age.

Must this grim scenario bear out? Not necessarily. Barbara Butrica and Eric Toder asked this question almost a decade ago. They found that without savings or access to defined contribution plans or pensions, the answer is quite often yes. However, they suggest that the answer is not always a simple yes. Using the Urban Institute's Dynamic Simulation of Income Model (DYNASIM), they projected that nearly two thirds of baby boomers with low earnings between ages 22 and 62 will end up with low incomes at retirement, but more than one third will defy the odds and escape poverty in old age. This latter group will be able to move up the income ladder in two main ways—continuing to work into older age or living with other individuals (often adult children) who help support them financially. And this difference in income is projected to be a significant amount of income—boomers who escape poverty as they age are projected to have an additional $8,400 in income coming from work earnings and $4,900 coming from co-resident income. In contrast, social security income—a major source of income for older adults—will be the same for all low-wage workers.[12] So a possible way to address poverty is just to not stop working or be fortunate enough to find others to share your living expenses.

However, this neoliberal perspective offers little wiggle room for individuals. Sadly, while it is promising that there are routes out of poverty, the routes Butrica and Toder found are solely based on individual responses—people must work longer or find family to live with. This is not always a possibility. Health gives out and one cannot work longer. This is especially true in the many physically demanding jobs that make up the low-wage labor market. While it may be easier to continue sitting at a desk and working at a computer as an older person, it is much harder in other jobs. Many low-wage jobs are physically intense positions that often involve standing for eight to twelve hours a day, working multiple shifts that disrupt sleeping patterns, and carrying large loads (be it patients, children, boxes, or trays of food). Over time these physical demands take a toll, leading to long-term medical problems that only magnify as one gets older. Ironically, the older Americans who most need to continue earning money as seniors are those who are least able to do so. And not everyone has family to live with to help share expenses. Of course, depending on individuals to find their own ways out of poverty is not something new in the United States. Our American Dream mentality is predicated on pulling oneself up by one's bootstraps, and our public-welfare policies have drastically migrated from a social understanding of welfare to a personal responsibility framework that blames individuals' lack of discipline and work for their current economic state.[13] As long as we focus on individual response (work more, save more, live with family), we do not have to address the larger structural constraints (low incomes in working years mean lower social security payments and ability to save). The decreased social safety net has had a drastic impact on economic security, and even low-wage workers who can save typically lack access to good retirement vehicles since many employers do not offer plans.

Inequality in the Low-Wage Labor Market

Since retirement is directly tied to labor market experiences, we cannot examine one without the other. Marianne Cooper has demonstrated that while retirement anxiety is felt across social class, the concern is most acute for those toiling each day in our low-wage labor market.[14] Low pay creates an economic insecurity that is just part of the challenge for workers in low-wage jobs. The low-wage job market is also characterized by a lack of health benefits and pensions, little control over one's hours, shift work that is often outside standard work hours, and little opportunity for advancement. This market has often been a trap for single mothers and women entering work after welfare reform. Women comprise 60 percent of the low-wage labor market, and they are employed in occupations such as retail sales, assistant positions, child care, waitressing, cashiering, fast food, bartending, home health care, housekeeping, and package handling. Indeed, as Joel Handler and Yeheskel Hasenfeld found when they examined the entire female labor force, close to one third of female workers are in the low-wage labor market (as opposed to one fifth of men) and earn less than $25,000 annually. In addition, low-wage work is just difficult to escape. While there is movement in and out of low-wage jobs, two thirds of those who moved to better-paying jobs returned to low-wage work, with women in particular exiting and then returning.[15] Of course, women are not evenly distributed in low-wage work. Instead gender intersects with race, ethnicity, and class to marginalize groups of women within low-wage work. Sociologist Evelyn Nakano Glenn's classic work in the 1990s found that white women tend to be in service jobs that are in the "public's eye" and require the most interactions and emotional labor; women of color are overrepresented in "dirty back room" jobs such as housekeeping and kitchen work.[16]

In her ethnographic account of luxury hotel work, sociologist Rachel Sherman found similar patterns today. She noted that hotel work is divided into two main categories: interactive and noninteractive. Interactive or "front-of-the-house" work consists mainly of intangible emotional labor, while "back-of-the-house," noninteractive work mainly involves physical labor. Sherman goes on to note that interactive workers are usually white (with the exception of bellhops and door attendants, who provide more physical work and are usually men of color), and back-of-the-house workers are typically people of color and immigrants. In addition, Sherman found wage differences with each category of hotel work. Not only were back-of-the-house workers paid less than front-of-the-house workers (about one to two dollars less per hour at the hotels Sherman studied), they also did not typically receive the tips that front-of-the-house workers received from hotel guests.[17]

However, these women (and countless others) exist not just in low-wage work but in the gendered and racialized nature of our labor market. When the economy dips, workers already in precarious situations are even more vulnerable. And for older workers—who may have a few precious years before their bodies fail them or they face age discrimination—the recession years are particularly economically devastating for them. This was highlighted in the recent economic recession as the public discourse directed attention to the impact of men in the Great Recession. This recession, like previous recessions, hit predominantly male sectors of the economy hard. Economists Heidi Hartmann, Ashley English, and Jeffrey Hayes found that about half of the job losses during the recession were in the manufacturing and transportation sectors (in which about 76 percent of workers are male).[18]

However, while job losses were higher in male-dominated industries during the recession, it did not mean that women fared well. In fact, the reality was quite to the contrary. Single women who were heads of households were almost twice as likely to be unemployed as married women or men—a rate of 12.6 percent. In contrast, the unemployment rate for all men was 10.5 percent; for all women the rate was 8.1 percent. During the recent recession, 13 percent of women who were the sole breadwinners for their families were unemployed, compared to 7.4 percent of married men and 5.5 percent of married women.[19] And across racial categories these disparities were even greater.[20]

Further, even when women held on to employment in the recession, they remained overwhelmingly concentrated in low-paying occupations. During the recession, the leading five occupations for women were (in order): secretaries, registered nurses, elementary and middle school teachers, retail salespeople, and cashiers.[21] Women remain in traditionally female occupations, some of which do not have career ladders, economic security wages, and pensions. And not only were women located in the lowest-paying occupations, they continued to earn less than their male counterparts across all occupations. During the recession, the pay gap stood at around 78 percent—with women earning 78 cents to every man's dollar. The pay gap existed across all categories of women—race, age, and occupation. And even when women invest in their education, that investment pays off differently for them relative to comparable men. The American Association of University Women (AAUW) reported that one year after graduating from college, women working full time earn only 80 percent as much as their male college-educated colleagues earn. The AAUW found that ten years after graduation, women fall further behind, earning only 69 percent as much as men earn.[22] So while women experienced less unemployment relative to men during the recession, they were able to hold their jobs, in part, because they are "cheaper" labor. Women work in traditionally lower-paying jobs, often without benefits and pensions, and even when they work alongside men, they are earning less because of the pay gap.

While fewer women than men may have lost their jobs during the recession, women were clearly being left behind when the economy began to show some recovery. From 2009 onward, men found jobs in sectors where women have not, and men have made stronger advances than women in other sectors. In particular Paul Taylor, Rakesh Kochhar, Daniel Dockterman and Seth Motel found that women lost a total of 433,000 jobs in manufacturing, retail trade, and finance during the recovery, while men gained 253,000 jobs in those sectors. And even in sectors where women had made inroads prior to the recession—such as professional and business services and education and health services—men did better than women. Specifically, even though 691,000 new jobs in those sectors went to women, men gained 804,000 jobs in those sectors. Meanwhile, not all women experienced the recovery equally, according to Taylor and his colleagues. During the recovery, the unemployment rate for black women grew to 14 percent, and for Hispanic women that rate grew to 12.3 percent. For white women the unemployment rate stood at 6.6 percent during the recovery.[23] The losses that women and people of color experienced during the recession are years of income and potential retirement savings that can never be recaptured—making the situation more desperate. Furthermore, this continues to exacerbate the wage gap across gender and race. So the lost and lower earnings of women and people of color during the working years contribute to lower social security payments in the nonworking years. Sadly, the wage gap is the gift that keeps on giving even after women leave the workplace.

While the gender and racial makeup of the low-wage labor market is a key feature for any long-term economic security, today's low-wage workers are much older than the average low-wage worker in the past. John Schmitt and Janelle Jones summarize the characteristics of low-wage workers by age and education, where low wages are defined as earning $10.00 per hour or less in 2011 dollars. Between 1979 and 2011, the average age of low-wage workers increased 2.6 years, from

32.3 to 34.9. The rise in the average age reflects a big drop in the share of low-wage workers who are teenagers—from over one in four (26.0 percent) in 1979 to less than one in eight (12.0 percent) in 2011. Over the same period, the representation of workers in the 25-to-34 and 35-to-64 age ranges both increased sharply. In 1979, workers who were 25 to 64 years old made up almost half (about 48 percent) of low-wage workers; by 2011, they accounted for just over 60 percent.[24]

Low-wage workers have earned higher levels of education than in years past. John Schmidt and Janelle Jones found the share of low-wage workers with less than a high school degree fell by half, from roughly 40 percent in 1979 to roughly 20 percent in 2011. However, the decline in workers with low educational levels corresponded with an increase in the portion of more highly educated low-wage workers. Specifically they note the proportion of low-wage workers with a high school degree increased, from 35.4 percent to 37.0 percent, and the proportion of those with some college education (but not a four-year degree) also rose, from about one in five (19.5 percent) in 1979 to one in three (33.3 percent) in 2011. And when we consider workers with a college education, we also find an increase. By 2011, almost one tenth (9.9 percent) of low-wage workers had a four-year college degree or more, up from 5.7 percent in 1979.[25]

In fact, in today's labor market low-wage workers represent quite a diverse group. David Cooper of the EPI notes that among workers earning $12 an hour or less, the average age is 36. A larger portion of these workers are age 55 or older (15.3 percent), compared to teens (10.7 percent). About two thirds of workers earning $12 an hour or less are age 25 or older. Not surprisingly, most low-wage workers (55.9 percent) are women; and more than one-third of low-wage workers are black and Hispanic workers. And the majority of low-wage workers (57.4 percent) work full time, nearly half (45.1 percent) have at least some college experience, and more than a quarter (27.7 percent) have children. In fact, nearly 40 percent of all working single mothers earn $12 an hour or less. These workers are, on average, the primary breadwinners for their family, earning more than half (54.3 percent) of their family's total income.[26] Many low-wage workers are trying to support families on these meager incomes.

Of course, one cannot divorce conversations about low-wage work from conversations about the decreasing value of the minimum wage. David Cooper traced the nominal and real value of the minimum wage from its inception in 1938 to today, as well as U.S. total economy net productivity indexed to 1968. He found that with the first increase following the end of World War II, the minimum wage rose rather dramatically in real terms, nearly doubling in 1950, followed by regular increases that kept pace with rising labor productivity until the late 1960s. The minimum wage peaked in inflation-adjusted value in 1968, when it was equal to $9.54 in 2014 dollars. Increases in the 1970s essentially held the value of the minimum wage in place despite higher inflation driven by oil and food price shocks. Yet in the 1980s, as inflation remained elevated, the minimum wage fell back to 1950s levels. Subsequent increases in the 1990s and late 2000s were not large enough to undo the erosion that took place in the 1980s. As of 2014, the federal minimum wage today is worth 24 percent less than in 1968. So Cooper concluded that low-wage workers are earning less than they did in 1968.[27]

Furthermore, the lack of economic mobility that characterizes so many workers' lives highlights the lack of routes out of elder poverty. If one cannot experience upward mobility in their working years, what chance is there for a secure retirement? University of Massachusetts economists Michael Carr and Emily Wiermers found that economic mobility—even for workers with college educations—has decreased from the 1980s. The found that "the probability of ending where you start has gone up and the probability of moving up from where you start has gone down."[28] *The Atlantic* summarized their findings with the forbidding headline "Poor at 20, Poor for Life."[29] Overall the American economy has been less conducive to mobility. The American Dream is more and more out of reach for so many workers. Part of the explanation put forth by Carr and Wiermers is that the number of jobs at the bottom of the labor market is increasing.[30] More and more workers are stuck in low-wage work for longer durations, and many for their entire working lives. They work but stay poor.

Inequality in Retirement

Not surprisingly labor market inequities are magnified in retirement. Monique Morrissey, a researcher at the EPI, issued an alarming report on the state of American retirement that found significant gender and racial differences in individuals' retirement planning. She found that the shift from defined benefit plans to defined contribution plans exacerbated racial and ethnic disparities. Up until the 1980s, black workers' participation in employer-based retirement plans was similar to that of white workers. However, black workers' participation began lagging behind that of white workers, and participation among Hispanic workers fell even further behind.[31] Morrissey and her EPI colleagues found that only 41 percent of black families and 26 percent of Hispanic families had retirement account savings in 2013, compared with 65 percent of white non-Hispanic families. And women remain quite vulnerable in retirement.[32] They generally live longer than men and are more likely to outlive their savings. Coupled with women's lower earnings during their working years, whatever savings pot they have (be it a defined contribution plan or social security) is already starting out at a disadvantage.

Inequality further shapes retirement prospects. For instance, the impact of gender seems to surface in two distinct ways. First, the less one earns, the less one can contribute to social security. Not surprisingly, women reported social security income that was lower than that of their male counterparts. Larger labor market structures—including occupational sex segregation and the gender pay gap—contribute to the concentration of women in low-wage work. And when we look across gender, it is clear that the gender pay gap haunts women in retirement. A 2015 report by the Women's Institute for a Secure Retirement (WISER) found that women are twice as likely as men to work part time, which means lower wages, fewer opportunities for promotion, a lower likelihood of pension coverage, and eventually smaller benefits.[33]

In 2014, almost 39 million women were paid hourly wages, and about 5 percent of women who were paid hourly rates had wages at or below the federal minimum, compared with about 3 percent of men. This phenomenon, the need for women to take time out of the paid labor market to care for their children, and the gender wage gap all impact the amount of money women are able to contribute to their social security fund. In this case, being a single mother limits women's labor market choices, forcing them to enter work that allows flexibility to care for their children, but not wages that offer economic security. In fact, the large proportion of women who lack economic security is largely attributable to gender differences in social security payments, which are calculated using which the worker's thirty-five highest annual incomes. Women retiring now began working in the 1960s, when women's opportunities were limited and they earned, on average, less than half the wages of men. Years of pay inequity add up to a significant difference in savings and social security payments.

To put this in perspective, Figure 1.1 shows the social security benefits earned by male and female workers in New Jersey from 2009 to 2013 who earned the median pay for their gender for all of their working lives, as compared to the Elder Economic Security Standard (Elder Index).[34] When the women retired, they collected just over $12,000 annually. Their social security benefits were $5,300 lower than comparable men's benefits of $17,300. As women age, the gap actually increases slightly with every social security cost-of-living adjustment. The wage gap in their working years continues into their social security years.

Second, some women also reported that, often following gendered expectations of women's roles in the household, they did not educate themselves on their economic security and planning for the future. As a result, they often found that they were ill-prepared when their husbands died. For instance, a retired woman I met from a middle-class background told me:

I'm in a position now that I am embarrassed about—never saved a penny; had no need to. I should have used my head. I had whatever I needed and wanted, and I lived a very happy life. No need to save to go someplace; we were a couple

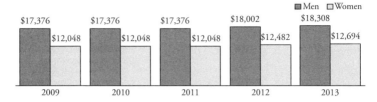

FIGURE 1.1 Gender Gap in Social Security Benefits, 2009–2013.

SOURCE: Jessica Horning in Mary Gatta, *Struggling to Get By: Elder Economic Insecurity in Bergen and Passaic Counties* (Washington, DC: Wider Opportunities for Women, 2013).

and went. I tell my children, don't do what I did; I am suffering for it now. I just don't have any savings. I don't know how to save.

One can be hopeful that as younger generations age, less rigid gender roles in families will lead to women exercising control over their finances, and the pay gap will start to diminish. However, a 2016 Wells Fargo survey of millennials (ages 22 to 35) found that the majority of women (61 percent) reported that their finances were stretched too thin to save for retirement, and 44 percent were not saving anything at all. In contrast, only 50 percent of men reported not saving.[35] Moreover, a 2015 study conducted by Fidelity Investments found that while 92 percent of millennial women want to learn about financial planning, 60 percent of those who wanted to learn expressed insecurity about doing so.[36]

In the same way that labor market inequities disadvantage women, they also disadvantage seniors of color. As Demos researchers Tatjana Meschede, Laura Sullivan, and Thomas Shapiro conclude: "Today's seniors of color spent much of their working lives in an era where redlining, segregation and labor market discrimination severely hampered their ability to accumulate asset wealth. While great strides have been made in the area of employment and housing discrimination in recent decades, the cumulative effect of such discrimination means that most seniors of color are facing retirement with few resources to meet their basic, everyday expenses."[37] They found that 4 percent of Latinos and 8 percent of African Americans are economically secure in retirement, contrasted with 27 percent of white households.[38]

The National Institute for Retirement Security found that workers of color, in particular Latinos, are significantly less likely than white workers to be covered by an employer-sponsored retirement plan—whether a 401(k) or defined benefit pension. They found that only 54 percent of black and Asian employees and 38 percent of Latino employees who are 25 to 64 years old work for an employer that sponsors a retirement plan, compared to 62 percent of white employees. This means that households of color are far less likely to have dedicated retirement savings than white households of the same age. And the racial difference is staggering: a large majority of black and Latino working-age households—62 percent and 69 percent, respectively—do not own assets in a retirement account, compared to 37 percent of White households.[39] The cruel irony is that the groups that fared the worst in their working years struggle the most in their retirement.

Clearly an analysis of the labor market, and specifically the low-wage labor market, must be part of our discussions about retirement insecurity. This book will connect these discussions—how can one think about retirement in a low-wage job, what happens when one can no longer work, and how do one's labor market experiences explicitly impact their retirement prospects. President Roosevelt stated upon signing the Social Security Act: "We can never insure one hundred percent of the population against one hundred percent of the hazards and vicissitudes of life, but we have tried to frame a law which will give some measure of protection to the average citizen and to his family against the loss of a job and against poverty-ridden old age." The stories in this book will share the reality of what Americans are dealing with almost a century after retirement security was first addressed systematically in the United States. And while the data illustrate that we have not lived up to President Roosevelt's vision, there is still a way forward for us to do so.

Book Overview

This book is about the lived experiences of workers struggling in low-wage work as they proceed toward an uncertain retirement. We look to restaurant workers as a classic example of unstable low-wage work that, for the most part, has not been associated with the kind of income or benefits that could mean a stable retirement. These stories exemplify the experiences of low-wage workers throughout life as they march toward uncertainty in their futures. The fact that this uncertainty is faced even by those who had well-paying jobs with benefits makes the challenges for low-wage workers seem insurmountable. This is the crisis that is upon us, and the catastrophe looming ahead.

What is it like to be staring down the retirement pike but still have decades to go? In Chapter 2 the stories of current restaurant workers illuminate their attempts to prepare for their economic futures in their thirties and forties—the Generation Xers. How do these workers define their economic situation, how do they see their future, and what are their plans for retirement? Concerns for retirement? Plans for their families? How do they envision their later years, including how long do they plan to work? Throughout this chapter, it becomes clear that Generation X workers—many of whom will not succeed at finding alternatives out of the service sector—will inevitably face economic insecurity, exacerbated by various health hazards associated with service-sector work.

"Lifer" restaurant workers throughout the United States bring another struggle as they try to make ends meet in Chapter 3. How can we understand the daily lives of these workers who spend so much of their working lives in low-wage work? What are the physical and health challenges of working in low-wage work and aging? What are the stereotypes of older workers? How do they balance work and family needs? How do they manage their economic stability? And it is important that we realize that this problem stands to get dramatically worse as the growing number of service-sector employees age.

The experiences of retired restaurant workers—many of whom are retired by circumstance and not by choice—are explored in Chapter 4. Many of the workers and retirees fear aging and retirement. For some, they may have mastered patchwork solutions to meet their immediate needs during their working years—by finding ways to get by and pay the mortgage or get food on the table—but have not saved enough money to no longer work. Others may have already outlived their savings, and others will never stop working. The stories of restaurant workers are complemented by the experiences of other retired seniors—some who had defined benefit plans and others who were surviving just on their social security checks. Almost all face economic anxiety at some level—and this chapter illustrates what it feels like to reach retirement age in economically insecure restaurant work. These points together make the larger argument that as more and more people enter low-wage service work and greater numbers of jobs outside low-wage work begin to mirror some of the worst workplace practices (movements away from defined benefit plans and decreasing value of wages), more and more people will experience insecure retirement across the board.

But the stories are not enough. Instead, it is through the stories that we can learn the lived experiences of workers and find ways to strategize about change and consider the policy implications of what we learn. What will the situation be like in 2035, when low-wage workers who are in their thirties and forties today will be approaching retirement age? Could the situation get worse? Is this the new normal? In my final chapter I address the larger concerns along with detailing a new social contract that involves public policy. How might workplace practices be reenvisioned? Can we learn something from the smaller portion of good service jobs? What new pathways to economic security in retirement for our aging workers can be put into place? This chapter provides the opportunity to reflect on the experiences on restaurant workers throughout the book and to use some of the higher-quality workplace practices in a small number of restaurant jobs to highlight a new social contract that can offer a path to an economically secure retirement for workers.

In all of this, a tension emerges between depending solely on an individualized strategy for any semblance of retirement security and having some social infrastructure and supports. Not surprisingly, having to depend on one's savings for retirement is often disastrous for many workers, particularly low-wage workers. In contrast, some social support—whether it comes from a partner's retirement account or a public program—can be significant in many cases. And this extends beyond the lives of low-wage workers. One backstory is not just in the potential retirement crisis for aging low-wage workers but in what this crisis foreshadows for the retirement realities for middle-class workers. As these workers increasingly experience many of the economic security challenges in retirement that low-wage workers have historically experienced, the numbers of workers struggling in old age will continue to grow. For current retirees—even those with union pensions—the economic realities are often too much to bear. In the next thirty years, those with middle-class jobs will be dependent on their 401(k) plans and may find themselves with debt from their working years. As they attempt to reconcile those experiences in retirement, they will often find these years filled with economic insecurity. Only by charting a new collective course forward can we help ensure that all workers can age into retirement with economic security.

CHAPTER 2

The Fast Money Trap

So, what is it like to be a worker in one's thirties and forties in restaurant work? These workers have spent two or three decades in low-wage work but still have a long path to a traditional retirement age. Referred to as Generation X, many of them entered the labor market in the 1990s and experienced more economic downturns than upturns. They are the generation who find themselves saddled with education debt, credit card debt, and housing debt as they attempt to traverse the labor market. By some estimates they report greater debt than other generations, and greater economic anxiety.[1] Within this economic context it is necessary to delve into the ways low-wage Generation X workers are thinking about and preparing for a life without work. What are their concerns? Do they share the same economic anxieties? Do they have safety nets or think that there will be any safety nets for them? Do they think they will end up "lifers" in low-wage work or are they trying to alter their futures? Here we meet workers who are still at least thirty years away from a traditional retirement age but already have spent a significant amount of their time in the industry. How do they conceptualize the connections between their working lives and retirement? What do they believe their futures hold?

The Economic Context of Generation X

Workers who are currently in their thirties and forties are commonly referred to as part of Generation X—the population born between 1965 and 1980. This generation completed degrees and/or entered the workforce during the recession of the early 1990s, experienced the expansion of a service-based economy and decline of our manufacturing base, and then lived through another recession in the early 2000s. Just as they were starting to make some progress—perhaps purchasing their first home or paying off their college loans—the Great Recession of 2008 hit hard. Many Generation Xers saw their jobs disappear and their houses lose value as the market crashed. Coming of age during the 1980s and 1990s when neoliberalism and trickle-down economics eroded worker protections, union density decreased, and pensions were replaced by 401(k)s, many of these workers began to believe that job security was a novelty. This was the labor market they were forced to negotiate and try to survive.

Research has found that overall, Generation X reports feelings of economic insecurity. A 2015 survey by Northwestern Mutual Life Insurance found that 40 percent of Generation Xers say they do not feel financially secure and 38 percent have more debt than savings.[2] Indeed, their financial security is amplified by the amount of debt they carry. Economists William Emmons and Bryan Noeth examined the inflation-adjusted amounts of household debt owed in the first quarters of 2000, 2008, and 2014 according to the age of the oldest person in the household and found that, on average, by 2008 members of Generation X had accumulated about twice as much total debt at a given age as birth-year cohorts observed at the same age in 2000. They found that the group with the greatest net increase in real average household debt relative to the life cycle patterns observed in 2000 were those born in 1970 (those who were 44 years old in 2014). The average debt of these households was $142,077 in the first quarter of 2014, or about 60 percent more than the inflation-adjusted household debt of the 1956 cohort in the first quarter of 2000.[3] They concluded that Generation Xers were significant borrowers during the years leading up to the Great Recession.

A 2015 Allianz Life Insurance study corroborates the fact that Generation X carries more debt than other generations: 38 percent more in mortgage debt (an average of $144,000 versus $90,000 for boomers) and 45 percent more in nonmortgage debt, composed of student

loan debt (an average of $12,000 versus $5,000 for boomers) and credit
card debt (average of $8,000 versus $6,000 for boomers). Further, they
noted that credit card debt shows a generational shift in individuals' use
of credit cards. The younger generation is using credit to finance their
lives. Nearly half (46 percent) of Generation Xers said they revolve their
credit card balances (only paying a portion each month), compared
with only 32 percent of boomers. Not surprisingly then, 48 percent of
Generation X members report that credit cards function as a survival
tool[4] that they use to cover living expenses.

The Pew Research Center has referred to Generation X as "America's neglected middle child"—bookended by the larger groups of baby
boomers and millennials. Generation Xers believe they will be the first
generation that will not experience social mobility relative to their
parents' generation. And when it comes to confidence about their retirement, they are more pessimistic than other generational cohorts.
Forty-four percent of Generation Xers do not think they will have
enough money for retirement, compared to 40 percent of baby boomers and 35 percent of millennials. Perhaps such concern is not surprising for the generation that had to withstand three recessions after they
entered the workforce and were the first generation for whom 401(k)s
replaced pension plans for most of their working years. And they are the
first generation predicted to hit retirement age just as the social security
program is projected to be exhausted in 2038—at which time it could
only pay 77 cents on the dollar of its benefit obligations.[5]

Within this economic context, how are Generation X restaurant
workers dealing with this reality? Some are trying to work harder and
longer. Following the spirit of the American Dream, they are hoping for
a good outcome if they do the "right" things. In some ways they are also
trying to create the social infrastructure that they believe they will need
on their own, not depending on a larger public support system. Others
are banking that their college degrees will finally pay off for them and
they will be able to find a job that offers them better economic prospects for the second half of their work tenure. Still others are embracing
a more entrepreneurial American spirit by finding traditional and non-

traditional routes to achieve professional fulfillment. Perhaps the one thing in their favor is time—particularly if they can work until their seventies. And since this is something that many of them believe they will be doing, they are trying to make that time work for them.

Just Trying to Make It Work

Central to the mythology of the American Dream is that if one just works harder, one will get ahead. Not surprisingly, one strategy among some Generation Xers was to try to "double down" on low-wage restaurant work, working more and more hours to make ends meet. Thus far though they were finding it a flawed strategy. They are putting faith in a system that has yet to pay off for them. For years they held on to a belief—the American Dream—that if they just worked hard they would be rewarded. Yet by the time that they reached their forties they simultaneously questioned that pathway while still trying to access some security within that system.

Jill, a 40-year-old white waitress from Austin, Texas, had already worked in the restaurant industry for twenty-seven years when I spoke with her. In high school Jill started working in a sandwich shop but quickly learned that she would have the opportunity to earn even more money in a tipped restaurant position. She started waiting tables at age 18 in San Marcos, Texas, where she worked two restaurant jobs—she waited tables at a diner in the morning and then worked as a cocktail server at night. "I was bankrolling. I was making hundreds of dollars a day between the two jobs." Jill then moved to Austin and continued to work multiple low-wage jobs, often working simultaneously at bars, restaurants, and coffeehouses. For fifteen years, Jill worked at least two jobs in the restaurant industry. As she approached her midthirties she was finally able to reduce her number of workplaces to just one—serving tables at a five-star restaurant in Austin. In Jill's words, "I fell in love with restaurant work there. I went to work each day and knew I was treating people well. This was my specialty."

She worked at the five-star restaurant for several years until, as she proudly told me, "I was poached from the five-star restaurant to run the front of the house at a new restaurant that was just opening." She learned, however, that the economic ladder she had counted on was not there. She was no longer serving tables, so she no longer made tips. Despite the title change, she ended up with a pay cut and was working more hours and harder for less money. For the first time, Jill had to learn to live off a paycheck. This had a significant impact on her economic survival plan. In the past her strategy had been to pick up an extra waitress shift if she needed extra money to cover rent or a bill. In her new position, that option was not there.

Then as Jill was progressing through her career she began to face serious health problems. At the restaurants she worked in, the managers would let the workers drink alcohol on the job. "Life got really crazy. I would get to work by eleven a.m.; by eleven thirty a.m. I would be handed a drink."[6] And often after work she would go out to unwind with her colleagues. The lifestyle—drinking, working long hours, lack of sleep—was taking a toll on her body and her finances. The challenge was magnified when she was involved in a bad car accident in which she broke her back. Jill found herself in a hospital and out of work. She had no health insurance but was able to access some charity care at the hospital. She left the hospital owing $45,000 in medical bills, about which she says, "I am just never going to be able to pay." By age 40 Jill found that the "working harder" American Dream mantra did not necessarily translate to financial security. She worked multiple jobs at once and even experienced career advancement. But she never was able to amass the savings to be secure and thus found herself living paycheck to paycheck. And the lack of benefits associated with her job led to insurmountable hospital debt.

Today Jill is trying to create a healthier lifestyle for herself while continuing to work in restaurants. She is back to waiting tables at a vegetarian diner in Texas that she describes as "fancy, organic, and local foods." She has a set schedule now, where she works from six a.m. to two p.m. each day. "It took a long time to get to this point. I took a pay cut to work in the mornings, but I had to for my mental health." In many ways, Jill is engaging in what sociologist Marianne Cooper calls

downscaling—emotional work that produces an attitude of seeming in-
difference to their future economic situation. At this point, Jill feels
her best option is one that she can survive in and try to "downscale"[7]
her economic worries for the future. In doing so Jill tells me that she
does consider herself to be in a "good place" now. Now that her lifestyle is better and healthier and she has control over her work hours, Jill
feels she has achieved success. And while she can make ends meet today
economically—as long as she ignores her hospital debt—it is question-
able what tomorrow will bring. She has chosen to live her life with that
doubt as one of her survival strategies.

Jill's story is similar to those of some other workers in their thirties
and forties with whom I spoke. Annie, a 37-year-old white restaurant
worker, bounced around for over twenty years waiting tables, bartending, cooking, and washing dishes: "You name the job, I have done it."
Like Jill, she spent most of her working years doubling down on restaurant work, often working two or more jobs simultaneously. And her
life followed other parallels to Jill's—she was in a serious bike accident
several years earlier and carries significant hospital debt. She has also
found herself homeless while working and has occasionally lived out
of her car. Jill and Annie also share stories of sexism and ageism in restaurant work. Having worked in both the front and back of the house,[8]
Annie notes, "Although there are more women in the front of the house,
that may not be the best career move." She feels that "jobs in the back
of the house are more dignified. It is easier to get that type of work as
you get older if you are a woman. In the front of the house, women get
viewed on their looks. I feel like I could continue to bartend until I am
in my seventies, but it is too hard to find work as you get older. There
are hundreds of young girls who would get a bartending job over me.
In fact, I was told at thirty-three years old that I was too old to bartend.
That is why I stay in the back-of-the-house jobs now." So while Annie
enjoys bartending, the nexus of sexism and ageism creates subtle (and
not-so-subtle) barriers to staying in that job.

Jill's and Annie's experiences of the intersections of sex and age discrimination in the workplace were a significant barrier to their economic

security. And while men also reported age discrimination, they did not experience the intersection of sex and age inequities. Of course, these intersections are not just in restaurant work or even low-wage work. Economists David Neumark, Ian Burn, and Patrick Button detailed overwhelming evidence of age discrimination against older women in the labor market. They designed a large-scale field experiment in which they created 40,000 job applications for job seekers and submitted them to a variety of online job postings. The résumés were stratified by age— older (ages 64 to 66), middle-aged (ages 49 to 51), and younger (ages 29 to 31) applicants. The economists found that the callback rate for middle-aged female applicants was lower than for younger female applicants, while the callback rate for middle-aged and young male applicants were about the same. The authors suggest that one possibility for this gender disparity is that women are subjected to an increased scrutiny based on physical appearance in the workplace.[9]

Jill and Annie found ways to work in the industry that are congruent with their lives, even though they must take pay cuts to do it—Jill looking for calmer front-of-the-house work in a diner and Annie securing less-lucrative back-of-the-house work. They spent years doubling down on low-wage restaurant work, which led them into deeper insecurity. They both felt that the doubling-down strategy was exhausting and often detrimental to their health. While they chose alternative routes in the restaurant industry, those new paths came with less economic opportunity. Both women found out how gender discrimination affected their ability to access better-paying work—a theme that pervades women's lives beyond low-wage work. And the pay sacrifice not only affected their ability to pay their bills, it affected their retirement plans. As Annie notes, "I worry about my future. I have no idea when I will retire, or even if I will." Jill, who also has no retirement savings, sums up her economic plan: "I have become skilled at being poor." Annie and Jill seem to be following a retirement path that so many low-wage workers face—entering retirement age without any savings and with significant debt, not thinking that there is even an option to retire, and trying to just work as long as they can.

So many workers engage in the emotional work of downscaling. As Marianne Cooper notes: "The downscaling of security involves lowering the bar on the requirements for security, resigning oneself to living with these reduced levels, and suppressing anxiety when it arises."[10] Jill held an even more nuanced view of her economic security. "What class am I? I am the service class with barter insurance. For example, when I broke my back, my restaurant friends brought me food. I was eating prime rib and lobster tails and not able to pay my rent." Jill finds that the barter economy is "something that workers are doing to survive." Annie also talked about bartering services—she would cook for a roommate in exchange for a couch to sleep on. In fact, Jill thinks that there may be a future path for her in bartering services. She is currently working on learning massage therapy in the hopes that she can barter massages for other services. She reasons that since so many restaurant workers don't have health insurance and are in pain after their shifts, they would need massages. This expansive understanding of the sharing economy offers hope to Jill as a route to support herself and her fellow workers as they age.

Jill's and Annie's stories represent a distinctive way to think about retirement. They frame their "downscaling" of worry within a larger context of agency and control. They suggest that they are choosing to take a pay cut at this critical time in their economic lives specifically because doubling down on low-wage work did not work for them. They see the exhaustion and worry that their co-workers in their fifties and sixties experience each day at work. And both women were not fully giving up on some semblance of security—they just were not looking for it in the traditional ways. They did plan on working longer but in ways that they felt would be more congruent with a healthy lifestyle. And they both believe that they have a network of friends and co-workers who will be part of their "tribe" as they age. They will all be in the same boat and together will provide for each other. In essence they have taken an individualized approach to creating a social infrastructure in order to survive in retirement. They believe that rethinking the sharing economy as a barter system in which they can share services, expertise, and resources may prove to be a way to better weather their economic insecurity. In that manner, perhaps the boat they will be on will not be a sinking ship. While their view is that their retirement will be more communal, they do not think there will be a government social safety net for them to call on.

Annie and Jill clearly illustrate how the traditional routes of retirement by doubling down on work—working multiple low-wage jobs to make ends meet or using a practice of "picking up" extra shifts to cover expenses—isn't a route to security. Moreover they have very little faith that a social safety net will be there for them in the future, so they are attempting to create one within their networks. They have not abandoned the American Dream, and in many ways they have embraced some of its major tenets—they just feel it is up to them to create the supports they need. Interestingly, their plan is not that different from that of some retirement communities that are emerging as the baby boomer generation finds the high costs of assisted living daunting. Creating intentional communities (from shared housing to multigenerational co-housing), many current retirees are choosing to live communally to take care of each other—emotionally, physically, and financially. These communities create the social infrastructure to address food insecurity, home health care, transportation, and belonging. Often referred to as a modern-day "Golden Girls" retirement strategy—those with little faith in the existence of public supports and not being able to afford private care—people are starting to form intentional communities to support a precarious retirement future.

Could New Forms of Work Offer Security?

While Jill and Annie represent workers who were trying to find security in restaurant work, other workers I met in their thirties and forties were attempting to make ends meet and build an economically secure future by taking part in the new and growing "gig" economy. The gig or on-demand economy represents a collection of markets that match providers to consumers based on need. Many people are familiar with the most common gig jobs—driving services such as Uber and Lyft—but the job opportunities exist across industries such as housecleaning, online selling, and shopping. In 2017 Bloomberg News ran an article titled "Six-Figure Earners Are a Growing Share of U.S. 'Gig' Workforce."[11] And while this is an enticing headline, the truth of gig workers appears far less promising.

A 2016 Pew Research report found that 24 percent of Americans earned money from the digital gig economy[12] in 2015. While Pew found that the median age of adults who are gig platform earners is just 32 years old, there were clear racial and income differences. Gig work is more prevalent among black and Latino workers than among white workers. While just 5 percent of white workers report earning money in 2015 from online gig work platforms, 14 percent of black workers and 11 percent of Latino workers earned money from the gig economy. Pew researchers noted that black workers in particular are more likely than white workers to have earned money doing physical tasks like working as a driver or by taking on jobs involving cleaning or laundry (5 percent of black workers have done each of these activities in the last year, compared with 1 percent of white workers). Further, lower-income Americans (those with an annual household income of $30,000 or less) are more than twice as likely to engage in technology-enabled gig work, compared with those living in households earning $75,000 per year or more.[13] Even the 2017 Bloomberg piece acknowledged this reality—the workers who are doing the best are not the new gig workers; instead they are "independent workers with specialized skills in fields such as engineering and computer science [who] are having little trouble finding clients as companies compete for talent in a tightening labor market."[14] And the end of the article states that for most workers, "on-demand jobs often lack the safety net of benefits and wage protections associated with traditional work arrangements. A 2015 report by the Government Accountability Office found that independent work tends to lead to fewer employer benefits and a greater dependence on public assistance than standard work."[15]

While gig work does not usually provide enough income to propel its workers into the six-figure tax bracket, it offers additional money that is critical to so many workers' economic survival. More than half of surveyed workers in the Pew study described the income they earn as being either essential to meeting their basic needs (29 percent) or an important component of their overall budget (27 percent).[16] This was also the case for some of the workers I interviewed. Darlene, a 45-year-old white bartender, spends her mornings working as a personal trainer and then spends her nights mixing drinks. She told me about the long hours and the disrupted sleep patterns. "I get off work at the bar around twelve or one a.m. and then try to get some sleep. And most mornings I am at a client's home by six a.m." Despite the grueling schedule, Darlene is not able to make her monthly expenses. The gig economy provides her with much-needed funds to meet her monthly expenses, not extra money that can be saved or make her wealthy.

Knowing her economic challenges, Darlene stressed how important physical fitness is to her. She shared that in addition to training her clients, she trains herself. She told me how important health insurance is through the Affordable Care Act, so that she can try to keep up with preventive health checkups. Perhaps not surprisingly then, she is less worried about her retirement and more worried about the here and now. "I look four times, maybe five before I cross the road, but there's a lot of seriousness to that. I get very concerned about getting injured when I'm off the job. Just little things like if I broke a finger or broke my hand, I would be in such a dire situation. It's funny, I almost feel like I can relate to a professional athlete who has to be so careful about everything they do because I know that if I'm hurt that I will have no income. That will be a huge, huge problem."

Darlene makes a conscious effort to stay in the present. She sees her jobs in the restaurant and fitness worlds as her only way to piece together her economic puzzle today. In her midforties she has no savings for retirement. However, she does feel like she as one asset—her health and body. She works hard to keep herself as healthy as possible so that she can work as long as possible (or even indefinitely). She told me there will be no retirement for her—she will always work. Income from work will allow her to pay her living expenses as she ages; she cannot afford to invest in a 401(k). Her plan is to keep herself as healthy as possible; her greatest fear is that something happens to her body or health that is out of her control. "There is no plan B for that," she tells me.

While Darlene uses her gig work to supplement her low wages and pay her daily expenses, other workers are putting their faith in the gig economy. Manuel, a 43-year-old Hispanic restaurant worker, started as a cook at a local pizza restaurant in high school. He then graduated, spent some time in the military, and returned to restaurant work in Florida, spending fifteen years at one steakhouse restaurant. He worked as a server, bartender, and then trainer, for which he traveled throughout Florida to train workers at restaurants that were just opening. Things were going well, but then his family moved out of Florida and he left with them to live in San Antonio, Texas. His company did not have a restaurant in Texas and he was out of a job. Luckily, he found a job at the airport waiting tables at a restaurant and then bounced to other restaurants. He was even able to get health care through some of these jobs, directly deducted from his paycheck. However, the health care contribution costs were too high for him to maintain. "Each week I would eventually owe money from my paychecks, so eventually I could no longer afford health care." Money was tight and he was forced to withdraw money from a 401(k) that he had amassed in his fifteen years working at the steakhouse. "I had to cash it out; I needed the cash to survive."

As he continued to wait tables, he began to experience increased physical pain. "Waiting tables is high energy and physical. As I was getting older as a server it was hard to change kegs, restock beers. I had lots of back pain. I just couldn't do it any longer." Manuel's health continued to get worse: "My mental health was bad. I didn't have a set schedule and my sleep was all off. I took sleep meds and it caused my nerves to get shot. I would dream every night that I was drowning, that I forgot a cup of soup for a table."

Eventually Manuel could no longer work effectively in the restaurants and he was let go. He received unemployment and food stamps and applied for the Affordable Care Act as he contemplated his next

move. In addition, his mother got very ill and he was a primary caregiver for her. "My schedule was not set in the restaurants, so it was so
hard for me to care for her." So Manuel had to find something different. "I found that I could promote websites from home and generate
income." He has begun this new "gig" and is hopeful that this is his
route to economic security. "I think it will take a year to build and then
I can make more money than in any restaurant job." Manuel is clear—
"I am fighting not to go back to restaurant work. I am banking on the
Internet and trying to build a business." Manuel has also started an IRA
to build his retirement savings back up. And working from home is allowing him to care for his mother more effectively. In fact, Manuel says,
"I feel great about the future."

Darlene and Manuel are looking at their futures in a slightly different way from both Jill and Annie. They represent a different perspective
on "doubling down" on low-wage work by using the gig economy as a
supplement to earn income or attempting to freelance as a way to escape the traditional low-wage labor market. This may or may not prove
to be a successful strategy and an actual route to some security. In the
gig economy there is no worker compensation, access to health care,
or paid sick days. Darlene's strategy is to keep herself fit and healthy
and take advantage of whatever health care she can through the Affordable Care Act. Manuel set up his own IRA, as gig jobs do not offer
employer-matched 401(k)s. These individualized retirement plans differ
from Jill and Annie's shared economy. Darlene and Manuel are banking
on a more traditional retirement path—work as long as one can and/
or save if possible—using the nontraditional vehicle of the on-demand
economy as one's income route and patching together gig jobs that offer
none of the traditional benefits workers expected decades earlier. Ironically, they are depending on the old models of work and retirement but
pinning their hopes on the new economy to somehow deliver on it—
perhaps putting them in an even more economically precarious position
both now and in the future. But the sense of agency and control that
the gig economy offers provides them some support. Indeed, regardless
of the path, these workers have embraced the neoliberal individualized

perspective on work and retirement. And the gig economy opportunities enable them to see themselves as more in control of their work lives. It is not clear, however, whether either the gig economy or the sharing economy will offer them any additional economic security, although it may offer some emotional security.

Trying to Create One's Own Ladder

While some workers doubled down on low-wage work, others felt that their only option to advance in low-wage restaurant work was to become a restaurant owner and create their own ladder of success. Some of this was rooted in their belief that an American Dream still existed at some level for them, and that their years of experience working in restaurants could translate into running and owning a restaurant. Management scholar Peter Watt argues that the focus on entrepreneurship as an ideal career route has its route in the American identity: "Entrepreneurial values have become part of the character of America and intimately related to our ideas of personal freedom, success, and above all, individualism. It is in this capacity that entrepreneurship is the fundamental domain in which the promises of the American Dream see its realization, and make up the interconnecting fabric that brings a nation of individuals together."[17]

Leo, an African American cook in his early forties, told me that owning a restaurant would be his next logical step. "I've been doing this for years and I love it and I am damn good at it. I am not leaving the work. Eventually, you know, I want to have my own business dealing with the food industry." Leo felt that his experience in restaurants was his greatest asset in starting a business: "Me being older, it's like I know, I've seen a lot of different personalities. And I've I have worked with good people, I've worked with bad people; great chefs with nasty attitudes, some poor chefs with great attitudes. And, you know, the ones that last are the nasty ones. Because there is a certain mysticism about restaurant work because you are literally catering to other people. It's like a customer service job. You are giving them some food and they are supposed to like it. It's perfection, it's precision, know what I'm saying, if you want the best quality, you just have to do the best. So, that's what I've learned." Leo very much captured a renegade entrepreneurial spirit—he felt that simply having worked successfully in the restaurants was enough expertise to run a restaurant.

Perhaps some of his confidence came from the fact that he was a bit more fortunate than other workers. Leo's wife had a job that provided health insurance, and the two of them have some savings. However, despite that safety net, he noted that it was not enough. "It's like we are putting enough away to have a tiny cushion. But we can't live off it; we are going to have to work forever." Just as for other Generation Xers I met, working longer remains a key feature of Leo's aging and economic security plan. Interestingly, Leo only saw ownership as the route to economic security. "But, you know, it is difficult; you just got to find your niche, get it and at that time, be your best at it, survive, and know that times will get better. You can't stay a bartender in a local bar all your life unless you own the bar. The same is true for cooks. You have to cook for yourself."

Yet despite having the drive to own his own restaurant, he did not have a plan. He talked about it as more of a dream, as the right thing to do to provide for his family. He had no idea about the capital he would need to start it up or even the type of restaurant he wanted. He only knew that if he was an owner he would be more secure. At the end of my interview with him I pressed him on this, and he seemed more reflective:

Mary: So your retirement plan is to own your business?
Leo: Hopefully. But who is to say that I won't be working for someone for the next twenty years.

In contrast to Leo, Sonja, an African American restaurant worker, has been actively working on her plan to open a restaurant in New York City that focuses on gluten-free foods. Sonja has worked for decades in both front-of-the-house and back-of-the-house restaurant work and feels confident in her knowledge of the industry. Sonja sees her entrepreneurship as her ultimate dream and has taken significant steps toward reaching that goal. "I am just clearing my credit report to bring up my score and would love to own and run my restaurant. I have written a business plan, I know how I want it to look, I have a name, I'm in the process of registering a name. I have a financial advisor and a mentor."

And while Sonja did not complete college, she has taken community college noncredit leadership classes in her spare time. In addition, she is actively branding herself as an "owner." On her social media presence on LinkedIn and other sites she describes herself as a restaurant entrepreneur. And although she is currently working as a waitress, she has set up an online site called Sonja's Sweets where she sells homemade desserts that are gluten free and diabetic friendly. She often sets up tables at festivals and public gatherings in her neighborhood to sell her desserts.

Interestingly, Sonja is currently an entrepreneur and in many ways has had some success. However, that success has not translated into economic security for her retirement, yet she feels that she is on a path that will. Still, she needs to keep her day job serving tables so she can build her business. Her overhead costs are now quite low—using existing social media sites (such as Facebook and Instagram) to advertise, preparing her desserts out of her home, and bartering services as best she can. Yet like Leo, she sees owning a restaurant as the only route to economic security as she ages. Sonja also is quite cognizant of how the structure of the low-wage labor market serves as a barrier to economic security in retirement. She sees her route to ownership as not just about her own economic security but also about that of others. As she develops her business, she is planning on taking what she knows about "good jobs" to her workers when she can afford to employ them—paying fair wages and helping to ensure that they have access to health care and retirement and that they work in a safe environment. She wants to be a good employer—to make the economic security opportunities better for herself and her workers.

Sonja, Leo, Darlene, and Manuel, while planning with different strategies, all seem to hold the similar belief that the existing system will somehow pay off for them. They have bought into the mantra that "working harder, working longer" will be the way they can succeed.

Depending on the gig economy or starting their own businesses, they view themselves as the drivers of their own destinies and see a free-market system both as the reason they have very little economic security today *and* as the vehicle for them to be economically secure in their retirement. This contradictory view may be an emotional coping mechanism, a larger sense of denial, or the impact of decades of socialization. Yet all four believed—at varying levels—that the system will work for them. And they held this belief despite the evidence in their own lives that it hasn't worked for them yet.

Leaving the Industry with a College Degree

While some workers are trying to find ways to stay in low-wage work, other workers I spoke with are planning routes out of it in order to achieve a semblance of economic security. One resource that some workers have to leverage is a college degree. We have all heard the stories of the college-educated Starbucks baristas or J. Crew sales workers. The Washington Center for Equitable Growth found that there is significant wage stagnation for college-educated workers, as the inflation-adjusted value of the wages of college-educated workers has barely increased in the twenty-first century. Moreover, the researchers found that between 2000 and 2014, employment of college-educated workers has increased much more rapidly in low-earning industries than in high-earnings ones. Analyzing the average earnings and share of workers with a college education or higher in ninety-one industry groups, they found that the industries with the lowest earnings for all employees are experiencing the largest increases in the share of workers with a college education or higher. In restaurants and bars, for example, 16.3 percent of all workers in the United States have attained a bachelor's degree or more in 2014, compared to 14.2 percent in 2000. In contrast, high-paying industries such as the financial sector saw their share of college-educated workers decrease, from 65.2 percent in 2000 to 56.1 percent in 2014. And despite the presence of college-educated workers, wages have not been boosted in these low-wage industries. The economists conclude that "the implication of these findings is that the U.S. labor market doesn't lack for college-educated workers. Workers who have degrees are already taking jobs further and further down the job ladder. Encouraging or subsidizing higher education attainment will not solve the fundamental problem facing workers in the current job market: There are not enough jobs."[18]

Denisa is a 38-year-old white bartender who started mixing drinks to pay for college. She graduated from a prestigious university with a degree in journalism and never envisioned herself tending bar as a career. When she graduated from college she took a job as a reporter in Florida. She was quickly promoted to associate producer and then news director within five years. The promotion, though, did not necessarily lead to a secure income. At her peak in the Florida news business she was earning $28,000 a year. As she says, "Granted, I was young and I took the job as a news director and part of the benefit is that I got to be a news director at a young age, but when it comes down to it, I could earn significantly more money as a bartender than I could as a news director at a TV channel."

Denisa then took a risk and left Florida to try to break into journalism in New York City. She took a night bartending job in Hell's Kitchen and did some voice acting during the day while trying to catch a break at news organization. The years went by and Denisa found herself bartending full time at age 38. "I did not expect I'd be in this situation. I try to thrive at whatever I do, but it's funny, I went to one of the best journalism schools and I was good when I was in daily news, and I somehow got caught in this cycle of bartending and I think it's because the money is there and it's also it's kind of a draining industry and you're constantly bouncing around. I am getting close to forty years old and I started getting very nervous about the fact that I need to really get out of this now."

While Denisa works at higher-end restaurants in New York City and New Jersey where she can make decent tips, there is no real sense of security. "On the Fourth of July I can make $800, but I'm working for thirteen hours, moving nonstop, exhausted. I mean, it's a very grueling job. It's not easy work and you really have to work it. But then I have days where it's completely slow and you can never predict what you're going to make in one week. . . . What's so annoying about this industry is you can go in one day and make hundreds of dollars; you can go in the next day and make $20." Denisa knows this is not a sustainable lifestyle: "I can't even think about marriage or children. I do not want to be a bartender when I'm married or have kids. It's not the kind of life—I mean, you're working evenings." However, Denisa does have some savings for her emergencies and her retirement, yet she fears that her options will be very limited as she ages.

The anxiety Denisa feels is shared by her family. She says, "My mother does not understand. She calls me every day and is practically in tears. At least four times a week we have a serious talk about how talented I am and how good I am at anything I do and then her next question is, you know, so what are you going to do with your life? And I mean it, literally I can't tell you the anxiety this woman goes through. She doesn't understand how I went to a great school, was good at what I did and how I'm bartending now and she doesn't like that lifestyle for me. I mean, I guess no one does." The encouragement from her mother helped Denisa develop an economic security plan. She is currently taking college classes to parlay her existing degree into a nursing degree. She expects to complete the program in the next year or so and then enter a job that can offer her a stable income and some security. Unlike Jill and Annie, Denisa is not downscaling her economic security. She is worried and trying to use the resources that she has—her existing degree—to find a path out.

Denisa also notes that her story is not unique, and the data on low-wage workers bear this out. "I know so many people like me—serving or bartending with college degrees. I don't think people have this idea in their minds, but you have a lot of people now who with the economy are having a really hard time finding jobs, and they may have a degree but can't figure out how to put it to use or they can't get hired and so they start working in this industry." In fact, one in eight college graduates are currently underemployed, according to an analysis of the 2016 college graduating class by the Economic Policy Institute.[19] That means that 12 percent of the college-educated workforce is working at jobs that don't require a college degree, working part time but wanting full time work, and want to work but are not currently in an active job search.

Denisa's assessment of her college-educated peers is a solid summary of Marcus, a 40-year-old African American waiter I interviewed. Like Denisa, Marcus hopes to parlay his college degree to get out of restaurant work. Marcus started in the restaurant industry twenty-three years ago, and he adamantly told me that he would not recommend that anyone go into the field. "The minimum wage is so low that I never get a paycheck, I only get tips." Marcus does have health insurance through his restaurant, but he must make sure he works thirty-two hours a week, which is challenging as schedules change often and workers may be sent home when the restaurant is not busy, thus losing hours. Marcus also talks about the wear and tear on his body over the years and his concerns about being able to continue the work. He also is keenly aware of how his race and age intersect to impact his income. "I am African American; I know I will make less than my [white] counterparts. And the older I get, the more people perceive me as 'lesser' a worker."

However, Marcus is also aware that for now restaurant work is the best career for him, specifically because of the workplace flexibility it affords. He and his partner had a son two years ago. His partner works days and since they cannot afford child care he must work nights. Being able to share the child care is most important right now, and restaurant work affords him the opportunity to work an alternating shift schedule with his partner. However, he told me, "When my son goes to preschool I am leaving restaurant work. I have little retirement savings; I need better for my family. I have a bachelor's degree that I completed in 1995 and I have done nothing with it. I don't know what I should do, but I know that I need to do something."

For low-wage workers who do not sense any ladders to move up, the solution may be to move out of low-wage work for more security. Workers with college degrees—many of whom may have taken lower-wage jobs in a tight labor market when they graduated from school—

are better equipped to parlay those degrees into better-paying jobs. The options they have may help them gain economic security over time. Moreover, Denisa's and Marcus's stories highlight how college-educated workers may also come with advantages in the low-wage labor market. Denisa works as a bartender in restaurants that offer the opportunities to earn higher tips. In many ways Denisa was employed in a restaurant where she could be economically secure—she earned more than minimum wage, had access to health insurance through her employer, and made enough tips to even put some money into savings. However, she felt that was not going to be enough for her to be economically secure. Her current work situation was better than that of many of the workers I interviewed, and her routes out were clearer to her than for other workers. Similarly, Marcus saw restaurant work as a way to manage work and child care demands (like many workers I spoke with) and also had health insurance from his employers, but even this did not downscale his worries for the future. Remarkably, Denisa and Marcus expressed the most worry for their futures, as compared to the other thirty- and forty-something workers with whom I spoke. Part of that may be tied to the view they both held: they had this resource of a college degree but felt that they were greatly underutilizing it. Having the degree seemed to amplify their concerns for the future—almost feeling as if it was a lost opportunity they had to recapture before it was too late. The question that kept them up at night was, what could that opportunity really be?

Rethinking the System: Making Bad Jobs Good

The workers I spoke with were trying to succeed—sometimes in creative ways—within the existing system. They knew that their insecurities regarding their future were rooted in the existing capitalistic system, but many still held on to the neoliberal American Dream story, despite the fact that they saw and experienced the holes in the story. Recall that Sonja's plan for her business reflected not only her vision that ownership of capital is her route to a secure retirement but that her business should support her workers' quest for economic security. Jill and Annie wanted to create a social network where people could care communally for each other—simultaneously rejecting the notion that aging is an individual act, while acknowledging it will be up to them as individuals to make that network happen. But what about the larger issue of trying to change the system; could this be a strategy? This more nuanced view indicates ways that workers can see their own individual responsibility for their future but also understand how changes had to occur in low-wage work to make economic security a reality. This vision was espoused by Jose, a 48-year-old Hispanic dishwasher in Chicago. Jose was born in Guatemala, where he was raised by his grandmother; he graduated from high school and worked as a television technician. He made a decent salary and could have a car and own a home, but ten years ago he decided to come to the United States to join his mother and siblings.

When Jose first came to the United States, despite his high school degree and technical skills, he could not find work in his field. He took a job cleaning offices but was laid off a few months later. A friend then told him about a dishwasher job opening at a local high-end steakhouse; he applied and was hired at $8 an hour. He noted, "It was such a luxury and fancy place that I thought working there would be so great." But he quickly learned that was not the case: "The work was physically difficult; I would work eight to ten hours a day in the same position, with no food breaks." As a result his arms and back constantly hurt. "I need pain relievers every day, but I take the Walgreens version because it is cheaper." And while he made a low hourly wage, that wage was compounded by wage theft. "The managers would punch me out before I was done. When I spoke up about it, they would give me the worse shifts. They then fired me one day for being late."

Jose then found work at another restaurant washing dishes, but the problems with his arms forced him to leave. He currently has no health care or retirement savings and is concerned about his future. However, his work in the low-wage restaurant industry has provided him with a pathway out. When I interviewed him he was just a few weeks away from completing his associate degree in sociology and had been working on local campaigns to raise the minimum wage in Illinois. His plan is to finish his degree and work in the social justice arena. He is clear that in order for him and his co-workers to be economically secure, the system must change. "We need actions to avoid more suffering and the lack of humanity. We have to provide good conditions to work. Why do so many of us have to work two or three jobs? The labor market is a slave system; the system decides and you are stuck. I want to change that."

The view that Jose holds is representative of a new way of thinking about work and retirement. And while Jose may be "all-in" about the need to change the system to have true economic security, many of the workers I spoke with also reported that the job quality needed to be addressed for them to have better economic opportunities—they called for higher minimum wages, paid sick days, paid family leave, real career opportunities, laws addressing discrimination, and health care. Some of them participated in social justice activities to address those concerns. Yet they still framed their personal retirement response as their individual problem and tried to make it work within an existing system. They often did not place their future economic insecurity fears or struggles within the larger context of the labor market, the decline of pensions and Social Security, or the broader neoliberal policies that make preparing for a secure retirement a challenge. In fact, instead of a critique of broader national policy, they felt that it was up to them to prepare for their retirement. They needed to find better jobs, work longer or forever, make a new pathway, or save more. Even Jill and Annie, who embraced a more communal and sharing economy for their retirement survival, still saw it as something they would need to create, not something that should be part of a new social contract. Jose's perspective that the overall policy and labor market system needed to be addressed for one's current *and* future economic security went further to challenge the economic system itself.

Conclusions

The restaurant workers in Generation X share many retirement concerns—little or no savings, significant anxiety about health care, the need to work longer than anticipated, and depending on others (such as family and friends) for their safety net. They also found that advancement in low-wage industries does not necessarily or neatly translate into economic security. Instead, they are forging ahead and attempting to create new pathways to survive. Some of them are embracing new modes of planning—trying the gig economy, living clean and healthy, creating a communal sharing economy, and engaging in social activism to help create opportunities and better jobs for workers. Others are taking more traditional paths to the American Dream—calling on the entrepreneurial spirit that is so often, but many times falsely, associated with economic security. Finally, workers with college degrees are trying to make those degrees work for them, while questioning if that is at all possible.

The workers I interviewed all coped with their existing and future economic insecurity by still believing in the American Dream and exerting control by attempting to live that dream in their own ways. They all had concerns about the point in their life when they would no longer be able to work. Yet perhaps because their march to retirement was still decades away, they felt, at some level, that they were going to be able to plan something. In the best-case scenario they do have many working years ahead of them during which they can save as much as possible for retirement. However, the feasibility of that individual savings for retirement in and of itself may just not be enough. With effective social and workplace policies and programs in place, it is not too late to positively affect their retirement prospects.

While middle-class families are surviving with more resources than many of the restaurant workers in their generation, the futures of these two groups are increasingly converging. Aging is a factor in everyone's retirement considerations, but it affects some more than others based on their ability to establish safety nets. Perhaps because I am part of their cohort, I wanted so badly to have hope for my Generation X peers. But throughout my interviews, it became increasingly evident that a new social contract—one that rewards work and broadens the safety net—would make such an economic impact on their lives, and the lives of all of us. The challenges that Generation X restaurant workers face as they contemplate retirement point to the significant challenges in retiring when jobs pay too little and lack key benefits. Yet meeting the Generation Xers in the restaurants reminded me how connected all of our futures are. Many Americans are expecting to live and work longer and have less savings than they need. Depending on one's network during aging is not distinctive to Jill and Annie but is part of many retirees' plans today. And many Americans—those in low-wage jobs and those in middle-wage jobs—raise similar anxieties about their retirement prospects. While the Generation X restaurant workers' concerns may seem more acute, the reality is that they are not that distanced from their peers in other jobs.

CHAPTER 3

Aging in Low-Wage Work

The workers we have met thus far had already spent decades in low-wage work but still had years of working ahead of them. They struggled to plan for their lives postemployment and felt anxious knowing that they have only a finite number of years left before they will be forced to stop. For so many low-wage workers in the labor market, retirement apprehension is heightened by a grim reality of deep economic despair. For those who can barely cover their life expenses while they are working, what happens when those paychecks stop coming? Up until that point the American Dream has meant a good-paying job, a home you could afford, and a secure retirement. What dreams are available to them when those three metrics are out of reach?

We have just considered Generation X workers and learned their struggles and fears about the year ahead. Now we move on to another group of workers—those who are at the point of retirement in the traditional sense. How is this crisis—impending for the workers in the previous chapter—already affecting older low-wage workers today? Americans got a glimpse of the reality that so many of these workers will be facing when a photo of Fidencio Sanchez went viral online in 2016. Fidencio is an 89-year-old man in Chicago who works every day pushing a frozen-treats cart in order to earn money to cover his living expenses. He told a local reporter that he needed to work because he had no retirement savings. Fidencio has been working since he was 13 years old but could not save for his "golden" years because his low-wage jobs barely kept him above water. His customers, however, wanted to help him and his family, and they set up a crowdfunding campaign to raise

$3,000 to help Fidencio take care of his wife, who had recently become ill. The campaign went viral and closed with over $384,000. All because of the generosity of strangers, Fidencio now had the retirement fund he could not afford to save for during his working years.

The circumstances surrounding Fidencio's story, how he got to the point of having no savings, are not unique. Unfortunately, most people in his situation are not lucky enough to receive the help they so desperately need. A 2016 study by The Associated Press–NORC Center for Public Affairs Research found that one quarter of workers age 50 or older say they will not retire. Among low-wage workers, earning less than $50,000 a year, the proportion was 33 percent.[1] So over a third of all low-wage workers will be in Fidencio's shoes when they are approaching 90 years old. And the difference is that they will probably not have a crowdfunded campaign to raise the money they need to retire.

These older restaurant workers throughout the United States have spent their lives in low-wage work. They struggle differently than the 30- and 40-year-olds do, as they have fewer years left to work ahead of them. They had not necessarily planned to spend their careers in restaurants, but they are now staring down into retirement and coming to grips with the economic and career contexts in which they have lived. What do the daily lives of aging restaurant workers today look like? How do we understand the lives of workers who ended up spending so much of their time in low-wage work? What are the physical and health challenges of working in low-wage work while aging? What stereotypes pervade the image of older workers? How do they balance work and family needs and manage their economic stability? We meet them next as they provide insights into their work and their lives.

Cooking Up a Future: Building a Career or Working Indefinitely

Sociologists Deborah Harris and Patti Giuffre note that in the United States the fascination with cooking and cooks is a staple of our American life. They note that "the rise of the Food Network helped make its cooking show hosts celebrities, providing more attention to those who cook for a living."[2] Many chefs from Anthony Bourdain to Rachael Ray to Andrew Zimmer have become household names and have helped to greatly increase the professional status of chefs. They note that "the rise of the celebrity chef serves as its own distinct version of the Horatio Alger story."[3] Author Gwen Hyman once said, "Cooking was the work of the hand that was also the work of the mind: the job fused artisanal prowess, creativity, discipline and professionalism. It required no advanced degree or business suits. . . . At the same time it held out, for those who succeeded, the promise of not only financial reward but also the patina of class."[4] The cultural attention to the top chefs in New York City or Los Angeles makes everyone believe that they too can achieve the American Dream in this career.

The real path to the American Dream is, however, quite different for most restaurant cooks. The success of Bourdain or Emeril Lagasse is often quite unique from the experiences of the cooks at your local Chili's restaurant, McDonald's burger joint, or neighborhood bar, and even among some of the higher end restaurants such as the Capitol Grill. Most cooks in kitchens are not the top celebrity chef, making millions. The U.S. Bureau of Labor Statistics reports that in 2015, the median pay for cooks in the United States was $10.44 an hour or about $21,720 a year. Bakers earn a similar annual income of $24,170, and even chefs and head cooks—the top earners in the kitchen—only earn a median income of $41,500.[5] Economic stability is not a centerpiece of this work.

Don, an African American line cook in his early fifties, has worked in restaurant kitchens for the past twenty years, with a brief stint working as a cashier in a fast-food restaurant. He is currently working as a cook at a nonprofit homeless agency in Manhattan. In fact, one of the reasons he took the job was that the nonprofit offered him health benefits. Previously Don had spent several years cooking at the concessions at stadiums throughout New York City. He enjoyed the work but found it to be an extremely unstable source of income coupled with very intense work demands. "It's very physical, the overall standing, moving around, sometimes you've got to lift certain amounts of stuff, forty pounds of sugar, ice, big cans. Lot of bending over, lot of stirring, strenuous work." And his income varied depending on the events at the stadium. "I used to work with a lot of older workers at Citi Field for the U.S. Open. Every year that was like their date night. During the year there was no regular job, but there might be benefits that they receive. But during those three weeks when the U.S. Open was in town, that's when the older people are sweeping, mopping. And then those three weeks become the money-making weeks." He equated the cycle to a drug addiction. "Once the U.S. Open is gone, all the workers are looking for the next fix. It's a vile cycle."

Don believes that the work as a cook at the shelter is a better fit for him. Like Jill, Don has chosen the importance of workplace environment and stability even if it means a pay cut. He takes a train from Brooklyn about twenty-five minutes to his job, and he has set hours of ten a.m. to 5 p.m. "I've got to just heat up a lot of the stuff or I might have to cook certain meals specifically for some of the clients. Because of their diet restrictions. And then at the end of the feedings, after serving the residents we clean up and get ready for . . . 'cause it's two shifts—it's lunch and dinner." And he takes great pride in his work. "See, the thing about working is that if you love doing it, it's not really a job. So what goes into the action of food is a lot of work. In order to have the best food or best work you have to be ready to put in that work. And me being an older man, it only helps me because it keeps me active and alert. It keeps me on point."

Despite the love he has for his work, it is still a struggle to get by. He knows that he is paid just over the minimum wage and below a livable wage for New York City: "I have a wife, she works; our combined salary helps us get over. But in the beginning it was hard, I was working for Citi Field and working only when there were home games. Money was sporadic; sometimes I had to get food stamps. You know what I'm saying." Perhaps even more unsettling is that he sees himself just staying afloat as he proceeds toward any semblance of retirement. "No support for my situation. You know restaurant work is, a lot of times if you are not a chef, sous chef, or something like that, then it's going to be hard for you to make that money." And while Don said, "I don't want to be working a strenuous job at sixty-five or seventy," when I asked him what he thought he would be doing at 75, he said, "I'll still be on the grill."

Like Jose the dishwasher we met earlier, Don believes that the larger system of work needs to be addressed—no matter how many hours or jobs he worked, it would never be enough. In fact, he felt that if public policies did not change, things were going to get worse for everyone. He is concerned about working while sick and notes that many cooks he knows come to work with the flu and other communicable illnesses because they do not have paid sick days. He adds that the minimum wage needs to go up in New York City. However, he laments, "The future is rough. But I look at it as all blue-collar workers and minimum-wage-area workers are going to have it real hard. Because they are not making ends meet now and the rent is going up, the food is going up, mass transportation is going up. So what're you going to do? You are going to be more dependent on the government. And the government isn't really interested in taking care of you, it doesn't really care. They need youth and energy. They want people for military. The revolving-door mentality, looking to replace. That's the bad part about it. People in legislatures are doing a lot of talking but not backing their words up. Even with the amount of people that come out in droves, it's like Marie Antoinette, they just want to give you cake, not real wages."

Don's frustration with government policies that have not protected him or his restaurant colleagues was painfully obvious as he spoke. He knew what he and his colleagues needed—a real living wage and benefits that could close the economic security crevasses in their lives. And without that, Don was clear that he probably will never be able to stop working. He knows that without the income from his work and his wife's, they will not be able to get by. There is no real retirement plan in Don's future; in fact, he even chuckled when I mentioned the work *retirement*.

However, Don is not discouraged. He tells me he will continue to fight for better wages and living conditions until his dying day. He spoke of his support of the Fight for 15. The Service Employees International Union (SEIU) and its partners' Fight for 15 has focused a national spotlight on the issue of low-wage work—highlighting low wages in fast food and other service industries, along with dispelling myths on the experiences of workers and focusing on the growing income inequality in the United States. Developing media campaigns and leading worker organizing and global strikes, the Fight for 15 movement has had successes: Seattle, San Francisco, Los Angeles, and New York, for instance, all adopted a $15 minimum wage, and Chicago and Kansas City adopted a $13 wage. They also have helped to increase minimum wages in other states. Don feels their impact in New York; however, nationally workers are benefiting. According to the National Employment Law Project's (2016) analysis of the Fight for 15, nearly 10 million low-wage workers—59 percent—will receive gradual raises to $15. And their impact is affecting some of the largest low-wage employers. McDonald's and Walmart announced modest raises to $10.30. Other retailers and food industry leaders including the Gap, Ikea, Target, and Starbucks followed with similar raises. And Costco raised its starting pay to $13.00.[6] This is the hope that Don holds on to as he cooks each day, that his "retirement" will be the opportunity to work on these issues, while still working his day job. And that combination, he believes, will make his "retirement" bearable.

In addition to misnomers about the economic success of cooking, assumptions are often made that if one can build a career in low-wage work—progressing for instance, from waitress to cook to management, they would be more economically well off. Presumably these workers would have climbed the ladder in the industry. However, in many low-wage jobs, there is not always a ladder to climb. This tension was highlighted in my conversations with Cheryl—a lifer in the restaurant industry. Cheryl is an African American woman in her fifties who started thirty years ago as a bartender and progressed to manager. Despite the career advancement, however, her income did not rise. As she told me: "I get $300 a week and I get taxes taken out of that and then taxes on my tips taken out of that too, so I end up going home with about a $200-a-week paycheck and I work maybe about forty-five hours a week. I'm not bartending so I'm not making any additional money and that's when it kind of hurts cause I'm spending a lot more hours to make the same amount of money." And what is even more concerning is that she works for an employer who offers benefits—health care and a 401(k) plan. However, Cheryl has opted out of those programs. As she told me: "I'm in management. I could get benefits from them but it would again come out of my paycheck, so it would just dwindle down more and more." So while the option existed for Cheryl in the traditional sense of retirement savings programs through her employer, she simply could not afford to save. Like Don, she has no plans for retirement, although it was something she would like. "Maybe I can cut down my hours in my sixties and seventies, but I can't imagine not working. How would I live?"

Working longer and even working indefinitely has become the plan for several of the workers I met. In some ways the workers in their thirties and forties had learned this strategy from their older colleagues. Yet they also probably learned the lesson that working longer is just not enough. Even having college and graduate degrees cannot always be enough of a resource to climb a ladder to economic security. Denisa and Marcus, the workers with degrees, were eager to find a way to turn their college educations into a resource that could pay off for them. But questions lingered in my mind—did they lose too many years working in lower-wage work without putting money into saving vehicles? Can having the degree and putting that degree to use in some way work out for them? I got a glimpse of what their future may hold when I met Tanya, a 56-year-old white unemployed restaurant worker, on a cold, rainy afternoon in New Jersey. I quickly learned that her story cast doubt on the rosy reality they were hoping for. Tanya shared that, as did so many others, she started working in restaurants to pay for her college and law school educations. She enjoyed the fast pace of the work and the cash she was earning waiting tables. In 1986 she graduated from law school with a focus on employment law. She took a job at the National Labor Relations Board (NLRB) in New Jersey and started off loving her career. She spoke of her passion for justice and helping workers. Working at the NLRB, she thrived in a job where she was investigating charges of unfair labor practices and protecting the rights of workers to act together. However as the NLRB was increasingly defunded under President George H. W. Bush, her job became more stressful each day. She remembers going into work each morning and finding a stack of files on her desk that she would have to deal with. With less and less staff to help, she began to find herself drowning in the work and experiencing exhaustion. She made the difficult decision to leave her job and her law career.

Tanya had a plan—she was going to go the "alternative route" to a teaching career. The Alternate Route program is a nontraditional teacher preparation program designed for individuals who have not completed a formal teacher preparation program at an accredited college or university but want to obtain the necessary training to become a state-certified teacher. As Tanya was working on her certifications, she needed a job to pay the bills, so she went back to what she knew—restaurant work. So in 1992, at age 32, she was a waitress again while trying to patch together the classes she needed. However, she experienced challenges integrating life, work, and school; school was the one to go. So while the plan was for waitressing to be a short-lived stint, in 2016 when she and I met for coffee, she was still in the restaurant industry.

Over the decades she built a career in restaurant work, and she does feel that her degrees and education provided her with a leg up in securing those opportunities. She advanced from a waitress, to a bartender, to a cook in the kitchen, to manager of a fine dining restaurant. However, in all these positions she did not receive health care, nor did she have any retirement savings options. And she was, as she said, "barely skating along." Like Cheryl's experience, her advancement to management turned out not to be as much of a financial boon—at the height of her management career she earned $10 an hour. "The servers and the bartenders with their tips earned more than I did." And she faced sexual discrimination and harassment as she advanced her career in restaurants. When the owner of the fine-dining restaurant promoted her to manager, one of the assistant managers told her, "I am totally against women in the manager job." She would hear other managers talk about how they "wanted to grab my ass and other waitresses' asses." And this hostile work environment increased as she aged. The older she got, she saw how gender intersected with age in the restaurant business, and often not to her advantage.

As in so many low-wage jobs where one sells "service," Dennis Nickson and his colleagues found that the skills that employers demand are social and aesthetic. Compiling survey data from retail, hotels, bars, restaurants, and cafés in Glasgow, they found overwhelmingly that both interpersonal communication and self-presentation were central to service work. Specifically, 99 percent of employers felt that social and interpersonal skills were of significant importance, and 98 percent of employers felt the same of self-presentation skills. Conversely, only 48 percent of employers reported that technical skills were important.[7] Indeed, the right appearance and personality took precedence over technical qualifications. Lynne Pettinger found that sales assistants are a critical part of the "branding" of retail stores, and that their social and aesthetic skills are central to their work. One of her interesting conclusions is that "fashion orientation is one facet of brand-strategy [used by the stores] and the ability to present a fashionable appearance is one of the skills needed by sales assistants in many stores."[8]

As she aged, Tanya was told she had less and less of the aesthetic labor needed. The fine-dining restaurant owner, despite the good work she was doing, would repeatedly tell her that men all look the same as they age, they all look professional, and women don't. She knew that how she was being treated was illegal; her law background made that clear to her. However, despite that degree, she was economically vulnerable. She needed the work to pay bills. Like so many women, she was trapped in a cycle of discrimination. Eventually she left the fine-dining restaurant and has had a hard time finding another job. She told me, "The older you are, the harder [it is] to get a job." When we spoke she had finished a seasonal summer job working as a caterer at a large outdoor concert venue—where she worked with a number of older workers, including a 90-year-old waitress.

Despite a lifetime of work and promotions, Tanya has no retirement savings and health care. "I think for so long I lived in denial," she noted.

"I don't think about it, but now I have no choice but to think about it." To try to make ends meet over the years, she lived with her roommate and friend, Bert. Bert, a 57-year-old white restaurant worker, has similar concerns for his future. Like Tanya, he has experienced age discrimination in recent years. He has arthritis in his knees and back, making each day of work painful. His employer has noticed the pain he is in, and "demoted" him to serving lunch instead of dinner because he is "not fast enough" for the dinner rush. Without the dinner tips he's been accustomed to earning, this change meant a clear pay cut. Tanya and Bert have implemented the co-housing sharing economy that Jill and Annie were planning. Tanya reports that without Bert to share life expenses, she would be homeless.

Yet despite their co-housing arrangement, Tanya and Bert don't know what the future holds for them. Without any savings and both closing in on 60 years old, their only option is to work. Unlike Don and Cheryl, they do not hold out much hope that they will be able to work much longer. Both are facing age discrimination and failing health, meaning the retirement strategy of "working longer" may not be the reality. Tanya and Bert also have a minimal safety net. And having a more robust net could make all the difference in their economic security. Ironically, a woman who started her career fighting for workers' rights finds herself over thirty years later in need of that justice for herself.

The stories of Tanya, Don, Cheryl, and Bert show that one can make career advancement in title—from bartender to manager, for example—but it does not necessarily correspond to an advancement in income or benefits. Stories like theirs are more and more common not just in restaurant work but in many other low-wage industries. Our "American Dream" mythology suggests that a low-paid minimum-wage job is just a stepping-stone to a better-paid job; it is paying one's dues. Well, Tanya, Don, and Bert, along with millions of other workers, have been paying their dues for decades in these jobs. Is it their own individual failing that they did not progress to better jobs? For many of the workers they did progress in their work but not in economic security.

Economist Ben Casselman, chief economist at FiveThirtyEight, argues that it is much less an individual failing and more a labor market failing. He notes that there was a time when minimum-wage workers saw some advancement out of low-wage work. In the mid-1990s, only one in five minimum-wage workers was still earning minimum wage a year later. Analyzing data from the Current Population Survey (CPS) and the Survey of Income and Program Participation (SIPP), Casselman found that by 2013 that number was nearly one in three. That means that one third of minimum-wage workers are still in minimum-wage jobs a year later. Moreover, he found a similar rise in the number of people staying in minimum-wage jobs for three years or longer.[9]

And perhaps even more importantly for the workers with whom I spoke, Casselman found that older workers bear the brunt of this stagnation. He found that for teenage minimum-wage earners (a group that is shrinking among the minimum-wage pool), most do move on to better-paying jobs relatively quickly. However even the traditional young minimum-wage worker is finding it harder to advance beyond a minimum-wage job. Casselman finds that more than a quarter of minimum-wage earners under age 25 are still making minimum wage a year later, compared with about a sixth in the mid-1990s. Despite the declining success of younger workers, older minimum-wage workers face the most difficult labor market experiences. Casselman's analysis found that "more than 30 percent of those ages 25 or older are still working for minimum wage after a year. And more than 20 percent of those working for the minimum wage in 2008 were still in such jobs after about three years. Even those who did get raises often didn't get big ones: Nearly 70 percent were earning within 10 percent of the minimum wage after three years."[10]

This suggests that workers who take low-wage jobs have a particularly hard time escaping them. And what does escaping mean? The workers had the skills to perform jobs that were higher level and/or supervisory. They performed the work. The problem is not their deficiencies but the labor market reward structure associated with the higher-level positions. It is not an issue of just providing training or education to workers. It is instead looking at what the internal career ladders are in low-wage industries and determining if such ladders exist. Cheryl, the manager, who was making about $300 a week working full time, worked for a single proprietor and confirmed a lack of real ladders and advancement. That is also are true for workers in the multinational companies that make up our low-wage economy. The reality is, as Pablo Mitnik and Matthew Zeinberg have noted, that these industries often have "poor-quality employment structures—in all of them the proportion of bad jobs is much higher than the proportion of good jobs. In addition, all of them but business services have 'downstairs' employment structures; that is, employment structures in which there are significantly fewer jobs at each wage-level compared to the level one step below."[11] So while one may get a title change, they may see no economic change in their own lives.

Cheryl, Tanya, and Don also continue to highlight how race and gender impact workers' economic security. Recall from earlier that close to 20 percent of restaurant jobs provide livable wages. Restaurant Opportunities Centers United (ROC United) research has found that fine-dining servers and bartenders in cities like San Francisco and Oakland can earn between $50,000 and $150,000 per year. However, most workers (80 percent) are earning poverty-level wages. Workers of color are concentrated in lower-level busser and kitchen positions in fine-dining restaurants, and overall in segments of the industry in which earnings are lower. For instance, a 2015 ROC United survey of 133 fine-dining establishments found that 81 percent of management and 78 percent of higher-level nonmanagement positions such as captain, manager, and bartender are occupied by white workers, a disproportionate amount of these male. ROC United researchers further found that after adjusting for education and language proficiency, workers of color receive 56 percent lower earnings when compared to equally qualified white workers.[12] The question that remains is what exactly is mobility in the restaurant industry and how does race and gender impact one's chances of mobility that ensures economic security. And then, of course, how do we ensure that the 20 percent of good jobs are the norm in restaurants, and, more broadly, what are ways we can improve jobs in other low-wage industries? Perhaps it is those changes that create better, fairer jobs in restaurants, retail, health care, and other service industries—changes that can ensure that workers who spend their careers in these jobs can afford to one day retire with security.

Can't Move Up; Make the Best of What You Have

If workers who climbed what little of a ladder existed struggled to make ends meet and had serious concerns for their futures, would there be any opportunities for workers who did not move to management? I met with Joan in her living room just a few hours before she was going to her bartending shift at a bar about a thirty-minute drive from her home in rural New Jersey. This was a commute that the 66-year-old white woman made six nights a week—arriving for her five p.m. shift and often leaving the bar well after midnight to head home. This grueling work schedule was not new to her. Joan had entered the restaurant business thirty-seven years earlier when she realized that her family needed extra income. However, she knew her work options were limited because she needed to work a job at night. Her husband—a roofer—worked days. She and her husband needed to split work shifts to manage the child care. As she joked to me: "Waitressing was the most respectful work I could find where every night I came home with cash."

Joan never imagined she would wait tables and tend bar for thirty-seven years. She laughed as she shared that when she took that first waitressing job, the hardest part was learning the liquor. She couldn't even draw on her own experiences, because Joan does not drink. She recalled: "I didn't know Beefeater was a gin, I thought it was a meat dish." She also remembered the first time a customer ordered a perfect Manhattan and how nervous she was to ask the bartender to make a "perfect" Manhattan. "I didn't want to offend him, I thought all his drinks were perfect!" Now, over three decades later, when I went to observe her at the bar during her shift, all her customers raved about her drinks. In fact, Joan's side of the bar was crowded most nights with regular customers who bemoaned that bartenders with Joan's experience and professionalism were a rarity today. Joan knows all her regulars' names, their life histories, and—perhaps more important—their drink orders. She bakes them Christmas cookies each year and brings them pumpkin bread in little boxes at Thanksgiving. She has seen many of them through divorces, family deaths, and job changes. As one of her regulars told me, "People come here for Joan more than they come for the burgers and beer." Despite the admiration and respect Joan receives from her customers, during her thirty-seven years of restaurant work, she has never earned the full minimum hourly wage, has never received health benefits from her employer, and does not have access to a retirement savings plan.

But this was not the life Joan thought she would have. When she graduated from high school Joan went to work at American Standard—a manufacturer of kitchen and bathroom products. This factory job provided her with a good wage, and she went to school at night to learn "keypunch"—using punch cards for data entry and programming. This precursor to the computers we use today, Joan felt, could offer her a pathway to a career, either at American Standard or at IBM—the latter where she set her sights on working one day. But Joan never got the opportunity to be an IBM employee. Life interrupted and she married her first husband a year after high school, and soon afterward she found herself pregnant with her first child. After having a second child, and with bills piling up, she took that first waitressing job in 1979. And then as she says, "You get sucked in and can't get out."

Several years later, at age 35, Joan had a new set of life challenges to deal with. She divorced her husband and was now a single mother of two. At that point, her dreams of ever returning to school were dashed. She talked about how hard it was during those years. Her children were still young and most nights she was not there to put them to bed. She was fortunate that her mother was able to provide child care while she was at work, and that every night she came home with cash. However, reflecting now, she noted that "the cash was a trap. You have to be disciplined with cash; it's not all good." And even though she had cash each night, it was barely enough to pay her bills. "At the end of the month, after I paid the bills, I'd be lucky if I had an extra $50. If I did, that was a good month and maybe I would treat the kids to a movie and pizza. Most times, though, we just got by."

It was in that restaurant where Joan met her second husband, Ralph. Ralph was a bartender, so while he also made cash each night, he had no health insurance or retirement savings. Ralph was the love of her life and they were married for thirty years, during which time things were good. They got by—no European vacations or fancy cars—but they paid their rent, put food on the table, and enjoyed their family. And they even put a little money away in a savings account. But then Ralph got sick and was diagnosed with terminal cancer. He could no longer work; he did not have access to paid sick days or private disability insurance. It was then up to Joan to make ends meet as a bartender, and they exhausted what little savings they had. She did the best she could to pay the medical expenses, but it was impossible. In fact, two years after Ralph's death in 2014, Joan still gets his medical bills. "All I can do is write back and say, 'He's deceased and there is no estate.'" What becomes clear from Joan's story is how her husband's diagnosis shattered her precarious economic security puzzle. Joan and Ralph could keep it together when they both were working and in good health; however, they were unprepared for the economic impact of Ralph's cancer.

Today Joan lives with her daughter and four grandchildren, and she is back to the "split shift" caregiving schedule she shared with her first husband over thirty years ago. She babysits her grandchildren all day while her daughter is at work, and then Joan heads to her bartending job Monday to Saturday nights. She has no savings left or retirement tucked away. As she told me, "I can never stop working. I have four grandkids that I have to help take care of. There is no retirement. I am hoping I can keep doing what I can do. Maybe if I can't bartend any longer, I can go to work at Wegmans." Joan does qualify for Medicare; however, the supplemental insurance costs her about $1,200 a month— something she struggles to pay for. As she quietly told me, "Getting sick is my greatest fear. I've told my daughter, if I get sick I'll jump off a bridge." So far Joan's been lucky—she has remained very healthy, with just some tendinitis in her elbow. However, she fears her luck will run out—and the only contingency plan she can come up with is death.

Joan is a lifer—she has spent most of her working years in restaurants, earning subminimum wages. Her goal every day was to earn enough to pay her daily expenses. When she was a single mother bartending in her thirties, a good week was when she could pay her bills and buy a pizza for her family as a treat. When she remarried and started putting a little money in savings, it got wiped out when her husband was diagnosed with cancer. Now she is helping to support her grandchildren and she still has no retirement in sight.

Despite the challenges, Joan has consistently focused on the positive. "I love my job. It's never the same things. I like what I do—so I am lucky. I can't worry about what happens next. I guess I could, but it would stress me out and it won't change anything." There are so many workers like Joan in the low-wage labor market—enjoying the work that they do but not receiving the labor market rewards to sustain themselves. Joan and her husband made it work for a good amount of time—they bore the brunt of the impacts of our public policies in their everyday lives. She addressed the lack of affordable child care by ensuring that she could work alternate shifts (first with her husband and now with her daughter). And she saved some money, but the health care costs of her husband's cancer wiped out that money. Had Joan had access to universal or even affordable health care, that savings fund could have been available to her to put toward retirement. She did what she needed to do to fulfill her end of the American Dream: she worked, lived within her means, and saved money. But there was no social contract to support her. It was the lack of a real social contract that contributed to her current reality where, at 66 years old, Joan is still struggling to pay her everyday bills and has mounting debt from her husband's illness. However, despite this, she is not worried for herself, but she said, "You know who I feel bad for, the people with the college degrees—more and more they are working in our industry because they can't find jobs. What will their future be like?"

Getting By, Until You Can't

Joan's story highlights how she will just get by until she cannot. She plans to work as long as possible, and because of that her nagging fear is less about money and more about her health. When her health goes, then what? This theme was shared by many of the individuals I spoke with—several talked about pinched nerves, bad backs and knees, and aching joints. Without health insurance during their working years and without access to paid sick days to even go to a doctor to have any of their ailments evaluated, their chances of ongoing care are low. As Joan said, her plan is to jump off a bridge if she gets sick. While clearly an exaggeration, the kernel of truth in her statement is raw. In fact, just as in the stories of the retirees in New Jersey and Massachusetts, health concerns and lack of affordable health insurance are often the trigger for an economic insecurity catastrophe. Retirees and workers can often "get by" if they are in good or even moderate health; it is when their health fails that the economic security crumbles.

The challenges of health and a lack of health care were most evident when I talked to a longtime restaurant worker. Becky, a 60-year-old white woman, has spent her life as a waitress and bartender, coupled with stints in retail work. Becky is a lifer who cycled through low-wage work, working in a variety of restaurants and retail establishments over her lifetime. She was married and divorced and found service work as the only route to make ends meet for herself and her two children. Because she spent her life caught up in a cycle of churning through low-wage service jobs, she consistently lacked economic security and she never had access to health care, paid sick days, retirement savings, and career advancement. But she was employed and worked consistently. When the Affordable Care Act became available, she could sign up and for the first time have health insurance. In some ways it was quite fortuitous—shortly after she was diagnosed with an aggressive cancer. Several weeks before our scheduled interview she was hospitalized in an intensive care unit. I spoke with her niece, Karen, who shared her aunt's story—one that was similar to that of so many low-wage lifers.

Karen told me that her father—Becky's brother—told Karen that "we are Becky's retirement plan." The family stepped up when Becky got sick and no longer could work. without any other supports, family is her only safety net. Her plan is that once she is released from the ICU, she will move across the country—from her home in Maryland to Indiana where Karen's father (her brother) lives. With Becky's deteriorating health, she is not expected to be able to work again, and without her family she has no other options, as she needs to live with a caregiver. Her economic security plan, like Joan's or Darlene's, was to get by as long as she could. But her failing health made her economic security plan fail. Because she had no access to health insurance or even a robust disability insurance program, the mounting health bills and her inability to return to work led to personal catastrophe.

What is compelling from the stories of the "lifers" is how they focused on individual options for their economic security during their working years and their "retirement" years (provided they can continue to work). Joan notes that she must continue to work—not just for herself but also to help her adult daughter make ends meet. Don and Cheryl plan to never stop working; Tanya and Bert are cobbling together whatever they can together. But the problem with these strategies is that they are individual-based and not sustainable. Age discrimination, failing health, and physical problems may make working until one's death impossible. Becky's story is particularly poignant as she is gravely ill and her family will bear the responsibility (both physical and financial) of caring for her. Their experiences are evidence of the clear internalization of neoliberal social and welfare policies of the last fifty years. In a society that views success and failure as solely the result of the individual, it is not surprising that individuals would search for individualized solutions to their economic insecurity.

These individuals and millions of others spent their working years in a climate of a fierce embrace of individual responsibility. Public discourse, dominated by attacks on welfare in the 1990s, led to the eventual passage of the Personal Responsibility and Work Opportunity Reconciliation Act (PRWORA) in 1996. PRWORA was a significant piece of legislation, premised on individual choice and responsibility and surrounded by stereotypes of people who were poor and just getting by, that overhauled the U.S. welfare system. The decades-old Aid to Families with Dependent Children (AFDC) was replaced with Temporary Aid to Needy Families (TANF), a time-limited system that requires recipients to participate in work or work-based activities to receive minimal cash assistance for them and their children. The 1996 law, publicized as "welfare reform," promised to "end welfare as we know it." Continuing into the twenty-first century, we have seen workforce policies slide toward a feeder into low-paying work and ultimately poverty.

In her ethnographic research of working-class men and women in Massachusetts and Virginia, Harvard scholar Jennifer Silva found that the workers she interviewed were "caught up in the teeth of a flexible and ruthless labor market that promises little job security, routine or permanence. In a time when individual solutions to collective structural problems is a requirement for survival, these men and women experience a common lack of resources—whether knowledge, skills, credentials or money—to protect themselves from economic and social shocks like unemployment, illness, or family dissolution."[13] This was the burden that the workers carried with them, especially those who were "lifers."

The Importance of Having a Safety Net

The lifers we have met thus far did not have robust safety nets. Government programs are not as robust as they need to be to cover the gaps lifers face in their economic security puzzles. Instead they depend on themselves and extended family to come back when they fall. What is it like to have a safety net? Like the others, Jim is a lifer in the restaurant industry. He is a 58-year-old white male who waits tables in western Pennsylvania. I met Jim through his work at ROC United, a part of the Dignity at Darden campaign.[14] The Darden Restaurant Group is the world's largest full-service restaurant group with over 1,900 restaurants and more than 150,000 employees in the United States and Canada, including popular chains such as the Capital Grille, Olive Garden,

Longhorn Steakhouse, Seasons 52, and Eddie V's. The Darden restaurants have been cited for particularly egregious labor practices. Per the ROC National Diners' Guide 2012, a consumer guide for ethical eating, many of Darden's nearly 150,000 restaurant workers still earn poverty-level wages with tipped minimum wages as low at $2.13 and nontipped wages as low as $7.25 an hour—$15,080 per year. Furthermore, Darden does not offer their employees paid sick days. Workers earning poverty-level wages simply cannot afford to take time off when they are sick—even though paid sick days would allow them to stay home when they are ill, recover, and protect consumer health. Jim is volunteering with ROC United on their Dignity at Darden campaign to fight for fair pay, health insurance, paid sick days, and other workplace policies to promote economic security among Darden's workers.

Jim proudly talks about his thirty years in the restaurant business. He started at a mom-and-pop restaurant as a waiter in college. However, like Joan, he lamented that "the pay in cash was a trap; when you are young it is good and tempting." So Jim dropped out of college and spent three decades waiting tables at a variety of restaurants in Pennsylvania—from Pizza Huts to high-end steakhouses and everything in between. He even left restaurant work for a short period to work in construction, but in the winter when there was no construction work available, he found himself back in the restaurant business and never left.

Unlike Joan, Jim can see that his health is deteriorating. "It's a young man's game—it's hard to keep up with the physical demands. The plates are not light and I am constantly carrying heavy loads." Despite the hard work, Jim keeps going. "I had a rotator sprain injury last year and I just worked through the sprain. I had no choice—if I didn't work, I didn't get paid." He told me that he is in constant pain and has tried to find ways to deal with the pain. He started going to the gym last year to try to get in shape, but so many of his injuries are cumulative, caused by years of hard physical labor. He notes that during his thirties, at one of his jobs he had to navigate two steps in the dining room. However, because they were so busy he would try to "jump" the steps to save a few seconds on each trip from the kitchen to his tables. That jumping years ago has led to an Achilles heel problem today. Each night after his shift he feels his feet ache as he tries to go to sleep.

Jim questions how long he can do this work. "I am coming up on sixty years old. I don't think I can keep it up. I don't know how much longer I can do my job. At my restaurant everything is refillable—bread, soda, soup, salad, pasta—it's like Whack-a-Mole. I just run my entire shift." And despite all this running, he has no idea when he will have a good night financially. "There is no steady income; my paycheck is minimal, maybe $15 a week. I am totally dependent on tips." The cash tips that were so enticing when Jim dropped out of college are now trapping him in a fluctuating income cycle.

However, Jim counts himself as one of the lucky ones. He has what he calls a "safety net." While his restaurant does not offer him a retirement plan or health insurance, his wife does through her job. "That is what sets me apart from my co-workers." And despite his "broken body," he loves the restaurant work. "It's flexible. I'm not a nine-to-five person; I couldn't have spent the past thirty years stuck behind a desk." His wife's robust employer-based retirement and health insurance puts him ahead of other workers. He is able to balance the unsteady tipped lifestyle with his wife's steady income and insurance. This partnership helps him feel secure and work in a job he loves. And the benefits from his wife's job also helps him cushion the impact of his deteriorating health, something that is distinctive from Joan and Becky's situations. Yet Jim, along with many others, conceptualizes a safety net in very individualized terms—having a partner who is fortunate enough to have employer-sponsored health care and retirement savings. Jim keenly understood this contradiction—and how lucky he was. He felt that he and his colleagues also deserved benefits. Like Jose and Don he was committed to work on social justice campaigns to change the larger labor market and government structures.

Career Changes Later in Life

Not all the older workers I met had spent their careers in restaurants. One of the more interesting bartenders I spoke with was Steven

O'Connor—who at 50 years old had just started working as a bartender four years earlier. Before slinging drinks, he was a broker and portfolio manager in a Wall Street firm in New York City. When the Great Recession hit, he lost his job at a hedge fund. He needed to find a way to make money and decided to try bartending. He had hoped that bartending would be a fill-in for a few months while he searched for stable work. And, like younger bartenders entering the field, Steven believed the cash each night was an opportunity to earn money quickly. He had never tended bar, but a manager at a local bar took him under his wing. He told me, "(The manager) said, 'O'Connor, that's a good Irish name, perfect for bartending.' " So he learned how to make drinks on the job, while trying to get back to Wall Street.

That was four years ago. Today Steven notes, "Yeah, well, bartending is my main source of income for the moment. I mean, what I do in New York City now is on such a smaller scale than what I used to do; you know, a guy got to do what a guy has to do to pay for the bills. Five years ago, seven years ago, I had the life of Riley. My hours were much shorter. I would be leaving my office at three p.m. and my income was ten times what it is now." And while he was able to make some inroads back into his old work in the financial sector, the work he is doing on Wall Street right now is 100 percent commission based, so there is no salary. So bartending, also a precarious income, is what he depends on. He sees the work experiences as similar in many ways—some days the bar is empty and some days it is intense. Like Wall Street, he notes, except for the money. He also notes that at age 46, when he lost his job, he realized it was not that easy to jump into new work. So bartending offered him an opportunity.

I met with Steven, recently divorced, in a condominium he rents with friends. Steven notes that bartending has a grueling schedule. After serving drinks all night he takes a forty-five-minute commute to Wall Street about four or five days a week. Sometimes he tries to work from home for his Wall Street firm. "Sometimes if I'm working too late at night in the bar I'll work from home just because I get home at two in the morning, and if I have to be up at five in the morning, I need a few more than three hours of sleep a night." He says the work is stressful and exhausting, but he tolerates it because of the need for the money.

The time behind the bar has changed some of his views on low-wage work. Too often, he says, bartenders are perceived to be unskilled, and that is not true. In fact, two years ago, while being interviewed for *Foreign Correspondent*, an Australian television show, on the lost American Dream, he told the reporter: "Five, ten years ago I would have been more of the pull-yourself-up-by-the-bootstraps kind of guy, but I guess my views have shifted definitely more toward the center. I think I'm more concerned with how other people are able to provide for themselves. I think it's a real big issue. Every family I know, all these people have two jobs."

Indeed, being part of the restaurant workforce created a situation that altered his view on the traditional American Dream. I asked Steven if he still believed what he reported to the Australian newscaster, and he said he did. People are still struggling today. He also said some of his former colleagues were trying to get into bartending. Using his economic skills from Wall Street, he told me that the projections are that food and beverage service is growing: "Maybe that's the industry to follow." While he didn't know how long he would be bartending, at the time of our interview he had no intention of leaving anytime soon.

Steven's story highlights a group of new low-wage workers—the downwardly mobile. The National Employment Law Project notes that the U.S. labor market is changing. During the recession, employment losses occurred throughout the economy but were concentrated in middle-wage occupations. Yet during the recovery, employment gains have been concentrated in lower-wage occupations, which grew 2.7 times as fast as middle-wage and higher-wage occupations. The lower-wage occupations that grew the most during the recovery include retail salespeople, food preparation workers, laborers and freight workers, waiters and waitresses, personal and home care aides, and office clerks and customer representatives. Overall employment has grown by 8.7 percent in low-wage occupations compared with only 6.6 percent in high-wage occupations. And middle-wage occupations have actually fallen by

7.3 percent. This uneven jobs recovery means that the "good job" deficit is greater than it was during the early 2000s.[15] Further, the proliferation of low-wage work is compounded by decades of wage stagnation. Over the past thirty years, the median wage for households has remained nearly the same. Indeed, the last decade actually saw a decrease in the inflation-adjusted average income for households. Available wages and compensation for most workers remains far below what should be expected given productivity gains and what families require to keep up with increases in the cost of health care, housing, and education.

This erosion of jobs is not surprisingly also leading to the erosion of the middle class, as more middle-class workers find themselves among the low-wage workers. In fact, per the Pew Research Centers, in 2015 the middle class reached a tipping point at which it no longer constituted the majority of the adult population. The researchers defined the middle class as households earning two thirds to twice the overall median income, after adjusting for household size. A family of four, for example, would be considered middle income if its total annual income ranged from about $48,347 to $145,041. Using this definition, they found that the shares of upper-income and lower-income households grew in recent years, while the middle shrank.[16] These trends certainly were pointing in this direction before the recession, as income inequality continued to expand over the past five decades.

These changes in the labor market are significant for middle-class workers, as they now often find themselves in low-wage work in the years that would traditionally close in on their retirement, offering a different perspective on working longer in the labor market. It also means that workers like Steven are entering restaurant work without having experienced the occupational health hazards associated with long-term work in the industry. Further, he has the advantage of savings from his previous job and some equity in a home, something that may be different from his restaurant "lifer" counterparts. This becomes a very different way of "working longer," as many large companies including McDonald's, Burger King, and Walmart have actively recruited older workers to fill jobs at low wages. And with those safety nets, workers like Steven can spend their later years in restaurant and retail work and may very well be more economically secure in retirement than workers who have spent their careers in those fields.

How Are Older Workers Marching Toward Retirement?

Older restaurant workers highlight the economic insecurity that many workers are facing. Like the workers in the previous chapter, these individuals spent much of their working years in the workforce. They have a strong work ethic and put in long hours. They work with aches and pains and juggle work and family demands. They challenge our stereotypes about low-wage workers—they are not teenagers earning extra money but parents and grandparents trying to put food on their tables. Some have college degrees and all have dreams for their future. They are proud of their work and spend their careers in their fields. However, the jobs they hold trap them in a cycle of working hard while still unable to get ahead. And although many older workers have been stuck in low-paying jobs for decades, others have fallen into the low-wage workforce after losing better-paying middle-class jobs. All the older workers I spoke with face the challenges of working while aging and the dire reality of having little or no savings for retirement. This means they need to make hard choices—trying to stay on the job sometimes well beyond an age where they can work; depending on friends and family; or hoping they die before they have to retire. In fact, the latter sometimes seems like the only alternative for some. The day after I interviewed Tanya, she sent me the following text message: "Hi Mary! I've polled some restaurant friends about their retirement plans and the consensus seems to be—hope I die before I get old. Crazy, no?"

The lifers are representative of workers who have spent their lives in low-wage work. They are the Fidencio Sanchezes found in every city and state in the United States. They work continuously for decades, yet they are not able financially to stop working, even as they approach their seventies. Evident in their stories is how the structure of low-wage work affects their economic security during their working years and diminishes their prospects for any real retirement.

First, the cash, on-demand economy where they have spent their careers makes any type of savings a daunting task. Like other low-wage workers, they do not know what their income will be week to week. "Volatile workplace scheduling practices" make it difficult to know when one is working and how much one is earning each week. This is particularly economically debilitating in restaurant work, as many of these workers depend on tipped income to survive. For front-of-the-house tipped workers, the tipping system itself makes it difficult to know how much money is available each month and makes estimating what percentage of one's income can be put into savings almost impossible. If workers are not scheduled for hours in a particular week or if a restaurant is particularly slow, there is no income. And the base wage is so low—the federal minimum wage is $2.13 an hour—that the prevalence of "void" or incredibly low weekly paychecks is the norm. This means there is no guaranteed income. Each workday is a gamble as to whether one will be paid.

Further, the tipping structure is increasingly a uniquely American workplace practice. The "anti-tipping movement" in the twentieth century in Europe and Australia, for example, led to a workplace where tipped workers were paid significantly higher base wages with no or minimal tipping. In contrast, in the United States, "the practice of tipping has been institutionalized through a wage system that not only creates a justification for the restaurant industry to not have to raise wages for its own workers, but also very nearly led to an industry arguing that they should not have to pay their workers at all."[17] The workers I spoke with spent the bulk of their working years without seeing a raise in this base subminimum wage. As a result of significant lobbying efforts from the National Restaurant Association, the federal minimum wage has been frozen at $2.13 an hour for over two decades. "The federal minimum wage has gone from $0 in the first minimum wage law in 1938 to $2.13 an hour over a period of almost 80 years."[18]

However, the same structure of unstable work schedules and income has been documented in other low-wage occupations that are not tipped, such as retail and health care. And as our "gig economy" continues to expand, with the growth of Uber drivers and other informal work arrangements, more and more individuals spend all or part of their working years in these contingent work arrangements. Recall workers from the previous chapter who hoped for a way out using the gig economy. Oren Litwin, author of "Reimaging Retirement in the Gig Economy," argues that the current retirement system does not serve contingent workers at all.[19] It is then not surprising that a 2016 Hyperwallet report found that nearly 70 percent of so-called "1099 workers"—which includes contractors and freelancers—have no long-term savings.[20] As Liz Ben-Ishai, a researcher at the Center for Law and Social Policy, succinctly stated, "Scheduling instability leads to income instability."[21] And this extends to one's retirement income becoming a challenge for more than just low-wage workers as more and more workers take on gig career paths.

So many of the jobs in the low-wage labor market often come without health care or retirement savings vehicles. And the way the wage structure is set—on low base wages, especially in jobs that are paid subminimum wages—there is very little to take out of one's weekly paycheck even if retirement vehicles are available. Low pay has a direct impact on the social security payments one can receive. It is clear then that the structure of work and low wages impacts one's future prospects. As these jobs continue to employ more and more Americans, workers will need different and innovative retirement plans if they are to have any savings at all. Work schedules and low pay must be considered not just in terms of the problematic nature in the here and now—making it impossible for workers to cover their daily costs—but also in terms of how this affects any conversations on retirement. This connection needs to be part of workers and employers' daily lives and underlie our public policy.

Conclusion

In this chapter we met workers who spent their career toiling in restaurant work or entered the industry later in life. Many of these lifers struggled to meet their basic expenses and expressed genuine fear about their futures. Some certainly tried to plan ahead and others were just now facing their futures. And even those who could save a bit of money often found it wiped out with an unexpected health crisis or job loss. Retirement was in their sights, but few could even imagine it a reality in their lives. Many of the lifers also defied the classic stereotypes of the low-wage workers: they often worked more than full-time hours and were supporting families as best they could on their wages, and some of the workers had college degrees. Yet it was painfully clear that hard work and even degrees did not shield them from a lifetime of low wages. Some workers tried to advance in the industry, only to learn that there was not always a ladder to climb. Often those who fared the best had some sort of individual safety net—a partner or spouse who had retirement and/ or health care coverage, or savings from a career prior to entering restaurant work. Yet even with those safety nets, while economically more secure, some still expressed some anxiety about the future. When we think about traditional work trajectories, the lifers in this chapter would be considered marching toward the end of their work lives, although all told me that they would not be able to leave their work anytime soon. They had spent decades in low-wage work, which made the prospect of retirement a real impossibility. They could not afford to meet their expenses without work. And compounding their challenge was the fact that they had spent the bulk of their work years in an economy where real wages began to stagnate and income inequality grew. By the time they reached a traditional retirement age, they could not retire.

CHAPTER 4

Retiring in a Coffin

In 2014 the satirical online newspaper *The Onion* ran a story with the headline "More Americans Putting Off Retirement Until Final Moments Before Death." They wrote: "Retirement is different for everyone—some people finish up working and then live off Social Security benefits for a few moments before passing on, while others may be able to lead active lives that last a whole afternoon. After a lifetime of working tirelessly to support themselves and their families, being able to enjoy several dozen seconds of retirement is a much-needed reward for most Americans."

Of course, good satire makes us think as it exaggerates our reality. However, the *Onion* piece is not a large exaggeration. As illustrated thus far, for too many workers, retirement, in the traditional sense of letting go from a lifetime of work, is simply an elusive dream. Working longer and indefinitely has emerged as the key strategy underlying most low-wage workers' retirement plans. Here we meet six retired restaurant workers, as well as retirees outside of the restaurant industry. The restaurant workers are not, however, retired in the conventional sense. None of the six retirees I talked to voluntarily entered the retirement phase. They only defined themselves as retired because they are not working and are well past traditional retirement age. Two were forced into an early retirement because of illness that prevented them from being able to physically work. And four of the workers found themselves retired because they lost their jobs—most commonly because the restaurant they worked at closed; all four are still actively looking for work.

The experiences of the retired restaurant workers in this chapter mirror, in many ways, the experiences of other retirees outside low-wage work. Therefore, I will juxtapose the experiences of retired restaurant workers with those of retirees (outside restaurants) in New Jersey and Massachusetts with whom I met in a series of focus groups. These retirees ranged from former union workers to low-income workers living in senior housing. What is striking is that the stories of the retired restaurant workers are not that different from the experiences of retirees who did not emerge from the low-wage labor market. Currently more than one in every eight people, or 12.9 percent of the population, is over age 65. By 2020, there will be 54,804,470 Americans age 65 and older, and by 2050 that number will grow to 88,546,973.[1] Throughout this chapter I intersperse the experiences of retired workers in New Jersey and Massachusetts as they attempt to attain a sense of economic security in their retirement years. The focus on New Jersey and Massachusetts was a deliberate choice. With a median budget shortfall of more than $10,000 annually in 2014, seniors in Massachusetts were the most economically insecure in the nation, and New Jersey seniors fell close behind.[2] Since these older adults have the largest gaps to cover, focusing on seniors in these states is a starting point for understanding that economic insecurity today is critical. By conducting focus groups with these retirees I identified the differences in their struggle to cover basic needs. How are they surviving? What sacrifices are they forced to make? What is the role of public supports in closing the economic security gap? What are their concerns for their future? And what does this foreshadow for all of us?

While we know that economic insecurity exists across demographic groups, gender, race, and income levels, it is important to understand how the mechanisms of social stratification—such as health disparities, structural inequality, culture, and social networks—organize the daily lives of older Americans. Differences across social groups demonstrate how the experience of aging is a critical part of our dialogue about inequality.[3] All the seniors you will meet in this chapter—whether they are restaurant workers or not—report significant concerns and anxiety about their economic situation, and they all engage in financial coping strategies to get by. However, the financial resources one can amass directly impacts those coping strategies. Those with some savings and pensions are clearly doing better than those who have little or nothing. But even having savings and income in retirement often proves to not be enough. And gender is critical here as well; older women—having been underpaid for most of their working lives—face even greater economic challenges in their later years than their male counterparts.

One finding that is critically important for today's retirees is that public supports are essential to their economic well-being, but such supports are often inaccessible or woefully inadequate to cover their needs or bridge the gap between their current incomes and future economic security. The retirees in this chapter are living embodiments of the changes in the retirement and economic systems over the past decades. Many find themselves at the edge of potential "benefit cliffs," where a slight increase in their social security income could cause them to be ineligible for another benefit, creating an even more precarious economic situation as they age. As public supports continue to face decreased funding, meaning that there will be less and less available to future retirees, how can those who earn less and can save so little be expected to age with any semblance of economic security?

This chapter provides a sneak peek at what could lie ahead not only for the older workers we met earlier but also for the rest of us. The stories of solidly middle-class union retirees struggling to make ends meet leads one to question how those without robust retirement pensions can survive. The seniors who are grateful for their subsidized housing (many waiting over a decade for it to become available) are clearly a cautionary tale for those who will be retiring in our age of austerity. What is perhaps most disturbing is that the coping strategies of today's retirees may be nowhere near the dire choices tomorrow's retirees will be facing.

Retired and on the Verge of Homelessness

Diane, a tiny 69-year-old white woman, met me at a coffeehouse in her town on a Tuesday morning. We spent much of the day talking about her fifty years working as a waitress and hostess in restaurants along the New Jersey shoreline. Our first meeting was at a café, an especially significant location given that her first waitressing job was at an all-night coffeehouse back in 1968. At age 18 Diane began waiting tables at the Poet's Corner, a coffeehouse/diner in a small New Jersey town. She worked five nights a week from seven p.m. to six a.m. For each shift of work she earned a base pay of $6.50 a night, plus tips. Diane worked at the Poet's Corner for close to twenty years, leaving in 1985 when a change of management made for a toxic workplace. In 1985, at age 35, she jokes that she was the oldest person working at the Poet's Corner. "I remember thinking what an old waitress I was then . . . and I was just thirty-five. But in the field even then that was old." She invested close to two decades in the restaurant and the new owners gave her a small severance for her loyalty. "It was pretty small, but I was still grateful. It was something."

Over the next few years she bounced from restaurant to restaurant, trying to find a good job with a sense of family and collegiality. In 1989 she found a job as a hostess and waitress at another local family-owned restaurant. She was making $125 a night as a banquet server along with her tips. It was good money and she had good co-workers. As she said, "I thought I would die there." And she did spend a decade working there but in a twist of fate, the owners—whom she considered family—sold the restaurant, and the new owners bankrupted it. At age 50, Diane found herself unemployed again.

Diane spent much of her career loyal to her employer—she had significant longevity at each establishment, spending the better part of three decades with just two employers. She also considered the owners as family—she poured her heart into their businesses and even babysat their children. In several ways, Diane is very much the ideal worker—loyal, committed, and productive. Like some many of the workers we met, she believed in the employment system. She felt her labor helped build the business and that the owners would always reward and protect her. However, the relationship was thoroughly one-sided. Over the thirty years she worked "off the books"—which means that for the bulk of her working years she never paid into social security, and there were no benefits—health insurance and retirement—associated with the work. Diane worked diligently for thirty years and had nothing to show for it.

Then in 1999 Diane's luck began to turn around. Her friend found her a job as a hostess in a new restaurant. She applied and was hired. It was her first time "on the books." In fact, she did so well that the owners started training her for management. For six years she worked as a manager earning $13 an hour and had employer-sponsored health insurance. Each year she got a Christmas bonus of $2,500. But then in 2005, that familiar story repeated itself—"some guys from Wall Street bought the place and ran it into the ground." The restaurant was located on prime real estate and the owners were able to sell the building for a good price. Diane, in contrast, found herself unemployed again. However, being on the books this time, Diane could collect unemployment. "I was so grateful that they let me collect." And for a few months she got by on unemployment checks and cleaning houses on the side.

Diane knew she had to find new work and again, on the recommendation of a friend, got a waitress job at a luncheonette across from the beach. For seven years she worked mornings serving breakfast and lunch to local fishermen and boaters until Hurricane Sandy tore through the Jersey Shore. Four feet of Atlantic Ocean flooded the restaurant, and it closed for good after the storm. And to make matters even more dire, Diane worked "off the books" at the luncheonette, so she could not collect any unemployment insurance. Fortunately, she was able to get a hostess job relatively quickly at another restaurant that fared better in the storm. Yet like at many seasonal restaurants, she worked more hours in the summer than in the winter. And years of this cyclical work schedule led to Diane claiming bankruptcy at age 68, as she had accrued significant credit card debt for the winter months when work was slow. At some point she was just not able to catch up with the debt. She used credit cards to pay rent and purchase groceries, as it was the only financial strategy open to her. Sadly, this is not a strategy unique to Diane. Over the years Americans at all income levels have experienced greater access to credit and, as a result, have increasingly used that credit to cover their basic expenses. Christian Weller found that credit card debt levels relative to income are highest among low-income families. These families, Weller notes, owed the equivalent of 9.5 percent of their income. In contrast, middle-class families owed 5.2 percent of their income and the highest-income families owed 2.3 percent. Further, Weller and his colleagues found that debt for low-income families was tied to purchasing life necessities or financing large-ticket items (such as trips or televisions).[4] Credit cards were a replacement income for many low-wage workers like Diane—leading to financial disaster.

Diane put her economic future in the hands of an unforgiving labor market. Her reasoning was economic survival—just trying to make ends meet each day, putting away what she could, and hoping for the best. As a result, reflecting back on her life, she laments how quickly the years went by and how her concerns for the future were no longer something she could avoid. And, more importantly, she found that "doubling down" on low-wage work—working harder, more hours, and more jobs—was simply not a winning bet, despite the fact that it is often accepted as a common policy response. If one just works harder, they will achieve the American Dream by pulling themselves up by their own bootstraps. This individualistic perspective often leads to an American nightmare as one ages.

When Diane and I met, less than a year after her declaring bankruptcy, she was again unemployed. She had lost her hostess job because of an on-the-job injury. She had climbed a ladder to clean the blinds at the restaurant, fell, and broke her wrist. When her wrist healed, her job was no longer available to her. Forced into retirement, she is still actively searching for work, applying everywhere she can: retail stores, beach clubs, and restaurants. Age discrimination, however, is the most significant barrier in her job search. She even took out an ad on Craigslist to pet-sit for local families.

Like Joan and so many others I met, Diane had not thought her life would be spent in low-wage work, nor had she thought she would be living in poverty as she turns 70 years old. After high school she had planned to go to airline secretarial school but could not afford the tuition. So she took that job in the coffeehouse in 1968 and found herself still in the field many decades later. When we talked about what comes next, Diane began to cry. She never owned a home, was never able to save, and had very little in social security payments each month. She was now two months behind in rent and her greatest fear is homelessness—and while she is on a waiting list for senior housing, that can take years to reach fruition. Her plan—if she loses her apartment—is to live in her car with her cat. Indeed, her one hope, if she cannot find work, is that she will get a settlement from the restaurant where she fell and broke her wrist, and that settlement will carry her until she finds work or dies.

As is clear from Diane's story, working after retirement is not always an option because finding a job as one ages can be very difficult. Maria Heidkamp and her colleagues at Rutgers University's John J. Heldrich Center found that older workers who are unemployed are less likely to find new employment than are unemployed younger workers. Many older workers involuntarily work part time because they cannot find full-time employment. Others become discouraged and drop out of the labor force, believing they will not find new jobs. Heidkamp found, through surveys and interviews of older workers, that they believed that age discrimination was a principal factor contributing to their failure to find a job. And as we saw in an earlier chapter, the point at which one is considered an old worker is getting younger and younger. Perhaps more concerning is that respondents in their late forties and early fifties cited age as the reason for their continued unemployment, and while acknowledging that the weak economy was a contributing factor to securing a job, respondents viewed age as the primary reason for not finding work.[5]

But job discrimination is not the only reason one cannot work into their golden years, casting increasing doubt on the working-longer theory. Many of the jobs workers had were physically demanding, and it is not always possible to keep up that work for the rest of their lives. A 2010 study by the Center for Economic and Policy Research found that nearly half of all workers over age 58 had physically demanding jobs.

That's eight and a half million people for whom work is causing pain and illness.[6] And that assumes they can continue to stay in these jobs as the demands of that work put even more pressure on their bodies as they age. Economic Policy Institute economist Monique Morrissey painted a grim picture on a recent airing of NPR's *Marketplace*. She noted that raising the retirement age will only leave more people in an economic limbo: "People won't be able to retire, but they won't be able to work either. And they're just going to be poor. I think we would have a huge, huge increase in poverty and near-poverty in old age." This was evidenced in my focus group discussions with retirees in New Jersey and Massachusetts. Several of them shared that their plan was to find another job after retirement, but they were unable to do so for health reasons. Some seniors had strokes and heart problems, preventing them from taking on work in their retirement or forcing them out of their jobs early.

While clearly many individuals in this book need to continue to work through their golden years, it is not a viable long-term solution. Real income needs in retirement are unattainable without work income. In most states, seniors need significant sums of money just to make ends meet. Take Massachusetts as a case in point. An analysis by Wider Opportunities for Women found that housing and health care costs comprise over 60 percent of the statewide average Elder Index budget. Just putting a roof over one's head is difficult. Nearly 45 percent of all Massachusetts elder homeowners, with or without a mortgage, devote more than 30 percent of their household income to housing expenses, and approximately 22 percent put more than half of their income toward housing. And while rents vary greatly in Massachusetts, senior renters generally experience challenges in affording their rent. In counties with the least expensive rents, typical economically secure seniors will allocate more than 36 percent of their income to rent. In counties with the most expensive rents, typical economically secure single renters will devote nearly 49 percent of their spending to housing. Such high rents make traditional measures of housing cost burden difficult to apply; for example, over 25 percent of elder renters spend more than 50 percent of their budgets on housing, far above the statewide average Elder Index and dramatically higher than the

25 to 30 percent of income typically cited as an appropriate proportion.[7] As Diane's story demonstrates and the data from Massachusetts makes clear, retiring from low-wage job (or even a middle-wage job) does not promise economic security. And the fear of losing one's housing looms large, forcing retirees to make hard choices or find new solutions.

Like Diane, 75-year-old waitress Anita finds retirement after restaurant work a delicate balancing act. Anita worked as a waitress in Maine for forty-two years—entering the waitressing world at age 32 when she found herself a divorced single mother. The hours in the restaurant suited her child care: she would work the breakfast and lunch shifts and then be home for her children. As Anita told me her story she recalled how she loved the work and got to meet incredible people over the years—she became friends with her customers and co-workers, forming a social and care network over the years.

Anita earned a low base wage and made most of her money on tips. "In those days you never declared everything; I had no idea it was going to hurt me in the future. I never thought about that. Instead it was like, I made thirty dollars this week, I can treat my kids to new shoes." So Anita never saved for retirement and never had any employer-based benefits. However, Anita never kidded herself that aging was going to be easy. "I always knew I should find something better, but I guess I was lazy or just never knew how." She never finished high school and always worried that her lack of education would be seen as a major failing in her job search, "despite the fact that I am a good worker and can run circles around younger folks."

Anita also thought the restaurant and the community it fostered would help her with the aging process. "I know my kids can't help me. My daughter is barely getting by with her kids and my son moved to Las Vegas, but I always thought the community of the restaurant would be there." In fact, over the years she saw how the workers took care of each other. She told me about Brenda, a waitress who had a stroke at age 75. "The owner let her stay and hostess—she needed the money. She was slow but we would help her out." Anita and her co-workers took food to her home and helped her with cleaning. "We took care of her."

Anita, like so many others I met, felt that some type of "Golden Girls" community of friends would be a buffer for them.

Anita believed this shared network would continue as she aged. But the owner of the restaurant died and his children sold the building, so at age 74 Anita was out of work. "Sure, it would have been great to just retire, but who would pay my bills?" After months of searching she was not able to find a restaurant job despite having close to half a century of work experience. That was when her old restaurant network came back into play. One of her co-workers was very ill and his children were looking to hire a part-time caregiver, and they chose Anita. So at age 75, Anita spends thirty hours a week caring for her friend. As she says: "In many ways it is like we never left the restaurant. We are still working together and caring for each other." She is hopeful that the restaurant network will continue to be the care network as they all age. Because of this network, she is less afraid of aging without savings. "Hopefully between all of us pooling whatever we have, none of us will be homeless and alone." Anita, like Tanya, has put into practice the strategy that Jill and Annie (Chapter 2) are banking on—a self-made care network of friends. These workers see the importance of collective care for each other as they age, and they realized that on their own they cannot survive. However, they formed that collective care on their own, within their own networks, and without larger support.

Diane and Anita, like many of the workers in the previous chapter, also highlight the importance of emotional strategies to deal with retirement insecurity. As Marianne Cooper found, for many economically insecure families "the key to getting by is a security built on downscaling: paring down the thresholds for security, embracing the power of positive thinking and worrying about today rather than tomorrow."[8] This strategy builds resiliency but does not concretely translate to real economic security.

Aging with Supports

Diane and Anita represent the low-wage workers who are struggling in retirement with no savings and very little social security. They struggled in different ways—Diane using credit cards and risking homelessness, and Anita depending on co-workers and friends to form a care village. As has been the case with many others, both are highly individualistic responses to the larger structural concerns associated with aging out of low-wage work. Their reality and the strategies they employ are not, however, inevitable. I met Henry, a 73-year-old white bartender from Brooklyn, New York. He is retired but like the other older workers in this chapter is looking for work. Henry fell into bartending later in life, in some ways very similar to Steven, the Wall-Street-broker-turned-bartender from Chapter 3. He started his career as a certified public accountant (CPA) but left at age 33 because he did not enjoy the work, and he stayed out of the workforce for ten years. When Henry ran out of savings from his CPA days, he had to find work. Not wanting to return to accounting, he began bartending at age 43 and fell in love with it, spending the next thirty years tending bar in Manhattan, Coney Island, and Brooklyn—including many iconic New York City bars like the Old Homestead Steakhouse and Marylou's in Greenwich Village. As Henry recalled, "It was amazing being behind the bar in New York City; you had the whole world coming to your bar. I had a stage."

Over the years Henry rarely had health insurance, and he had no retirement savings. In between jobs, any savings he had acquired would be spent on food and housing until the next job. And because much of his pay was in tips, during his bartending years his social security contributions were minimal. Currently he is looking for another bartending job but is finding that many New York bars are looking for younger bartenders. "There was a time in the seventies and eighties where people were looking for mature bartenders," he says, describing his predicament; "now they want the youngest, newest model."

But Henry has one advantage that many low-wage workers don't—a rent-stabilized apartment with a rent reduction. His housing costs are $287 a month in Brooklyn: "I lived here most of my adult life and I can never leave." In fact, the housing subsidy is the most significant factor in why Henry says, "I don't struggle. I do live cheaply—no girlfriend, no car, no vacation, and no dinners out at restaurants. However, if I didn't live in the rent-stabilized building, I would probably jump off a roof." The stabilization allows him to live off his social security and some small family savings he inherited. He knows his situation is rare for a bartender. He cringes as he tells me about his friend Charlie, a 78-year-old who is still bartending. "Charlie is struggling, like so many of the older guys. So many of them are going to go out of work in a coffin."

Despite financially scraping by, Henry wants to find work in retirement. "I enjoyed bartending so much and it would be nice to have a little extra each month. But I am one of the lucky ones; I guess the world looked out for me." Henry is concerned about workers who are coming up the retirement pike. "You can't find a stabilized building in New York City anymore. What are people going to do?" One possibility that he thinks may offer some hope is eliminating tipping and raising the minimum wage. "In New York City they are talking about increasing the minimum wage and getting rid of tipping. You know, it may just be the best thing—then everything will be on the books."

Henry's subsidized housing is critical to his economic security. In fact, subsidized senior housing proves critical for many retirees. This support was evident in my discussions with many seniors who were residents of subsidized housing in New Jersey and Massachusetts. While feeling economically insecure, they did recognize that having access to subsidized housing made a significant difference in their lives. At the same time, they were quite cognizant that it was inaccessible to most seniors in both states. They often referred to it as "luck" that they were able to access a subsidized apartment, mostly because of the long waiting lists. As one woman told me: "People are lucky to live here. There's a lottery system. The supply is so much less than the demand . . . if you get a low number in the lottery, you're lucky. There is a lottery system—with eight hundred names on the list; if you're eight hundredth to be called, it's easily a ten-year wait. I am visibly handicapped, but there are only sixteen apartments accessible, so it's a longer wait." Another woman supported her point: "We live here in subsidized housing and we are lucky to live here for only thirty percent of our income. I'm eighty-three. I was born in the first Depression and grew up with that . . . I'm trained. . . . You live within your means."

Their statements highlight two important points. First, a decade-long wait list is not only way too long but also immoral; while seniors are waiting (like Diane), they are often struggling to put a roof over her head. Another woman clearly illustrated this: "To me this housing is a blessing. I lived with my daughter and son-in-law for six years waiting for an apartment here. . . . I wasn't myself. . . . This (subsidized housing) to me was a godsend. . . . My daughter and son-in-law live close by and help whenever they can." Second, it is not just the lack of low-income housing that is critical but the lack of subsidized, handicap-accessible apartments. This is a significant issue for seniors. As a woman with a chronic illness shared, "I was in the hospital and a woman who lived here said, 'Jane, I'm going to bring you an application because you can't live in your house anymore. . . .' I had stairs and too many things (blocking my way). . . . I waited five and a half years because I needed my unit to be handicap accessible."

Another retiree stressed the dire situation that seniors with disabilities experience. "Affordable housing is a disaster. What they consider affordable housing is about one half to one fourth of retired income. Affordable housing is about $1,800 a month. This is why I don't live in Boston. The greatest chunk of my disability goes to housing. I am pretty much one check away from being homeless. If I don't have my disability check on the first, I am in trouble. I pay $1,300 a month for rent. I gave my notice that I am leaving. I am going down to Florida because I cannot afford to live here. I want to get into housing as a disabled veteran, but I cannot because I have a partial pension from a previous job, and I am over income by a couple hundred dollars, which means that I can never go home again because I qualify out because I am making too much money, which is never enough. You are told that you are not eligible for anything, but you cannot afford to live where you grew up. It is really hard that I cannot live where I grew up. I live far away, but now I need to have a car. I would rather live in the city so I could use public transportation more, but I have to have a car and it is expensive." The economic challenges for disabled retirees tend to be compounded—and all too often the supports are just not enough. Moreover, earning slightly over the program limits further deepens their economic security. They are too secure for government supports but too insecure to economically survive.

Perhaps even more troubling is that while housing assistance is essential, it is not enough to ensure economic security even for seniors who have it. As a resident from the subsidized housing developments noted: "I live social security check to social security check, even here [in affordable housing]. Social security and two part-time jobs—one is ninety minutes a day, the other on Saturday and Sunday." Indeed, it cannot be understated just how critical housing assistance is for those living on so little. Figure 4.1 shows how important public assistance programs are to an elder female renter named Jayne who lives alone in Passaic County, New Jersey. Jayne's income is the average social security benefit for Passaic County senior women ($2,646 per month). Because she has less than $2,000 in the bank, she is eligible for food, prescription, medical, energy, and rental assistance, as well as a small property tax credit. Assuming she receives all the assistance she is income eligible for, which is very rare, Jayne will remain far below the economic insecurity line until she is able to obtain rental assistance. State rental assistance is significant to address the economic security gap—raising her from 56 percent to 99 percent of the Elder Economic Security Standard Index. Rental assistance is a powerful tool to aid elders struggling to avoid destitution, but it is in short supply: in Bergen and Passaic counties, only 6,300 federal housing vouchers are available in each county. Even with the laudable elder set-asides built into the state rental assistance program, which is much smaller than federal housing assistance programs, many seniors are unable to access this vital support.

As a result, seniors often need several kinds of support to help them move toward economic security. As one woman shared: "I broke my hip and came out of the hospital and had Meals on Wheels. . . . It was $1.25 a week—I was saving money! So there are little perks in this county . . .

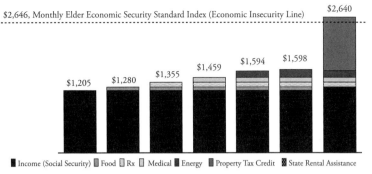

FIGURE 4.1 The Impact of Public Assistance on Economic Security for a Single Elder Renter Living on Social Security in Passaic County, 2013.

SOURCE: Jessica Horning in Mary Gatta, *Struggling to Get By: Elder Economic Insecurity in Bergen and Passaic Counties* (Washington, DC: Wider Opportunities for Women, 2013).

prescription, Meals on Wheels, and food stamps." Yet even when they have access to other supports, it often is not enough. "You get food stamps now, and then go to the market, and food has gone sky high. I get sixteen dollars a month; it's not what we need. If I go to the store and get a big packet of chicken, [that's as far as it goes]; nothing else."

While housing is a significant expense, so is health care. For all groups of retirees I spoke with, health care cost increases were a large concern, as was the lack of availability of public assistance to bridge the costs. Not only did health care consume a large portion of their income, but any increases in social security were eclipsed by rising health care costs. As one senior explained, "We get COLAs[9] on our social security, but this year only 1.7 percent. Our Medicare is going up by 5 percent. Our copays, if we have supplemental insurance, premiums go up every year. We are going into the hole." Another noted that "medical costs increase; just got a social security cost-of-living raise and Medco [a prescription drug plan] took it. . . . [the] raise was erased by the Rx cost increase."

Retirees also talked about how important transportation supports were for them, enabling them to attend medical appointments and do their food shopping. However, even with those supports there can be challenges. For instance, one woman reported challenges in accommodating aides on the transit that was provided by the affordable housing complex:

Transit is an issue; the bus can only hold so many, but that's not problematic. But it is a problem that only one handicapped person can go at a time. And if an aide is needed, they can't go with you on the bus; it's for residents only. They said it was because of insurance, and that it [transit support] is not for medical appointments—this is independent living, so transit goes to the mall and shopping center, but they try to accommodate if the doctor's office is en route.

This comment also highlights that having an affordable housing complex does not guarantee that a senior will have transportation for medical appointments. In those cases, senior need to plan ahead for transportation to such appointments. Yet even this planning comes with challenges. As one senior shared: "So transportation that you need to plan two weeks ahead for is [provided by the] township or county; it will take you to medical appointments, and I would have to have an assistant with me if I have a handicap of some kind."

Despite having access to some needed supports, retirees constantly lived with the anxiety that they would lose their public subsidies, either because their incomes would slightly increase, thereby making them ineligible for other support, or because the supports would no longer be there for them. This worry was most pronounced regarding housing. Subsidized housing is a support that cannot be understated in its ability to help seniors close the economic security gap. As one New Jersey retiree told me, "It's our whole life. If we were not living here . . . a lot (of landlords) want $1,500,[10] then a month in advance, etc. I worry if they will touch and change this housing assistance. Have to go forward and leave that alone. The concern is [that] our subsidies will be cut, [and] then [it will] cut into food, medicine, supplemental insurance."

All too often retirees not only live in households that lack economic security incomes, but many live with the anxiety that the public assistance on which they rely can be taken away at any time. Income eligibility limits for many assistance programs are intended to ensure that those with the lowest income get the most help. However, they also create "cliffs," incomes at which eligibility ends or benefit amounts decrease suddenly.

Thus, increased income may not improve a retiree's economic security but may even decrease it. Because there are fewer supports for those with incomes above the federal poverty line, many elders living above the federal poverty level find themselves almost as far from economic security as those living below the poverty line. Figure 4.2 shows the gaps between income and economic security across a range of incomes for elders who rent in New Jersey's Bergen County and do not receive scarce housing assistance. Because of benefit cliffs, a senior with $18,000 in annual income is nearly as bad off as an elder with $10,000 in annual income.

While concern for the potential loss of supports clouded seniors' lives, the real loss of supports was something many seniors had experienced. For instance, one man who has a disability shared how the loss of his home health aide had impacted his life. "When I came here, I had an assistant who would help me [with] doing basic things around the house, or using my car. The program was provided by the county. After seventeen years or so, they decided they would have to put an end on how many years you could get the assistance. They were erring toward younger people because they closed off the top end at seventy years old. I was well beyond seventy at this point, and it would now cost me $100 a day, and that I can't afford, so I am living in a slightly altered state today and some of the things I'd like to do, I cannot do."

Another retiree's electricity subsidy was eliminated when she did not use enough electricity in her apartment. "Now all of a sudden they cut

FIGURE 4.2 Annual Income, Maximum Public Assistance Available, and Economic Security Gaps for a Single Elder Renter Living on Social Security in Bergen County, 2013.

SOURCE: Jessica Horning in Mary Gatta, *Struggling to Get By: Elder Economic Insecurity in Bergen and Passaic Counties* (Washington, DC: Wider Opportunities for Women, 2013).

me off because I don't use enough electricity! Gas and electric gives you so much a month—say for six months. You don't have to pay your bills, so it's money in your pocket. Then they evaluate you again, and if you don't use a certain amount, they cut it off. I got a letter like that and asked them, 'Why are you penalizing me for using the electricity that the government pays for?' 'Let's evaluate you; okay, you don't have to use electricity.' I was just cut off; now I have to pay the electric bill."

Another woman noted that an increase in social security income created a benefit cliff for her that made her ineligible for the state prescription plan for seniors. This cliff made her even more economically insecure. "I had an increase in my social security income and it knocked me out of Pharmaceutical Aid to the Aged and Disabled (PAAD), and now I have to pay for my prescriptions, which I cannot afford."

One of the most severe stories a senior shared was one that demonstrated how waiting for Medicare eligibility cost a family member her life: "Within days, my son's mother-in-law and her husband both had had heart attacks. They lived on a farm and in order to pay the medical bills, the livestock, car, farm equipment, all had to be sold. The bills came in from doctors and there was still not enough money, so it wiped out their savings. A year later my son's mother-in-law developed cancer. She was a year out from Medicare. She decided to wait for treatment until [she was] eligible for Medicare and could afford it, and during that time it spread throughout her liver and kidneys. My son's wife was so upset; she screams she should never have lost her mother. If health care had been available for her, she would be alive today. At the end, she was just skin and bones; when she died she had just turned sixty-five, when she would have been Medicare eligible."

When One's Health Goes

Diane, Anita, and Henry all spent their careers in restaurants and wanted to continue working well into their seventies. But what happens when one's health makes the "working longer" strategy impossible? Tricia is a 55-year-old white restaurant worker who lives in Illinois. Tricia started in the restaurant business at age 14. "My family knew the owners and they gave me a job as a salad girl—I would make the salads and dressings." By the time Tricia was 16 years old she was promoted to hostess. "I was hooked on restaurant work." She then worked her way through high school and college as a waitress. After college she moved to Chicago and got a job as an assistant food and beverage manager. She then worked over the next twenty years in restaurant management as she raised her family. Then in her late forties she was diagnosed with cancer and got very sick. For over four years she battled cancer and could not work. She went on permanent disability and Medicare. However, despite her diagnosis, she tells me, "I feel blessed." Her husband, an environmental engineer, has both health insurance and retirement savings that she has access to.

Over the years of working and advancing up the ladder she only had health insurance and retirement savings from one of the restaurants in which she worked. Without her husband's savings and income, she does not know how she would be able to survive postcancer without work. "If I had to live off my disability payments, I think I would be so scared." In fact, Tricia has seen the impact of retirement insecurity in her own life and how retirees must work well beyond their retirement. "My father lost his job years ago, but in his retirement he needed to work to pay the Medicare supplement. So at seventy-six years old I got him a job in one of the restaurants I worked rolling silverware. He worked there until he died at eighty-two years old. He needed the money to pay for health insurance." Tricia also notes that "I don't know anyone who retires voluntarily from restaurant work. I know general managers in their seventies who are still working. I've heard colleagues wonder where they will live after retirement."

Another woman I met, Sue, shared a similar story. Sue, a 53-year-old white restaurant worker from Maryland, started her career as a fast-food worker in high school, and like Tricia she worked her way up the restaurant ladder. She loved working in the food industry and found the flexibility of hours very helpful as she raised her children. "I would work nights and my husband would work days. At the time I saw the flexibility as worth more than a 401(k)." And like Tricia, she had a husband with retirement savings and health insurance. "I was lucky, my husband had the job with the benefits. I couldn't have survived without him." While Sue is happily married, she acknowledges that divorce was her greatest fear. "I wouldn't have anything for the future." And her situation is not that different from others in the industry: "I know far too many great chefs without benefits." Sue also says that the restaurant business took another toll on her life. As she aged in the business she started getting ill—starting with premature contractions in her heart. After a series of doctors and tests it became clear that the stress of the food business—she routinely worked seventy-two hours a week—was too much for her body and she found herself retired on disability. And without the income from her husband, she would not be able to financially survive. As in Jim's situation (Chapter 4), Tricia's and Sue's partners provided the safety net during their working years and supplemented the disability and Medicare they received in retirement. Without their partners' safety net, both women would not have the additional income they needed to cover their costs as they were forced into early retirement because of illness. Neither woman could continue to work, yet neither had the savings on her own to get by despite decades of successful work in a low-wage industry.

Tricia's and Sue's stories highlight the concerns that older workers face in regard to their health. This was also true of the nonrestaurant retirees I met in my focus groups who raised serious concerns about the connection between security and health. Retirees having difficulty living independently because of poor health are most likely to have elevated health care costs and are highly likely to lack economic security. This group also faces increased challenges in trying to work as they age. Over 74 percent of elders who have difficulty with self-care are economically insecure, and nearly 71 percent of elders who report having trouble living independently are economically insecure.[11] Indeed, health care and medical expenses represented a significant portion of seniors' economic insecurity. As one man vividly shared: "I am Medicare away from being bankrupt. I can't afford Medicare Bronze, which is really the best. They force you to have these procedures and the cost keeps rising.

Who knows how much this whole thing is going to cost me? I have to pay twenty percent of whatever the cost is, and I don't know where that is going to come from."

So many seniors I met were deeply concerned about the rising costs of basic needs, most notably health insurance. And even those with secondary health insurance plans through their former employer and/or union did not feel this would be enough, particularly as they aged. One New Jersey man commented: "I have a fear. I have several health care conditions and if they deteriorate and I need constant care. . . . I'm not complaining, I have a pension, but home care is incredibly expensive." Income is important but not enough. Too often seniors found that health insurance—even good health plans—during working years did not translate into health insurance in retirement: "I don't have health care benefits. I was in a union for forty years—was in Amalgamated union. Nobody has benefits once they retire. You have to buy a supplement; it's expensive, and going higher." Failing health and health-care-related costs are a significant concern for workers and retirees. And the resources people need are not minimal. In 2017 the Employee Benefit Research Institute (EBRI) found that Medicare retirees need to have saved anywhere between $165,000 and $349,000 to *just* pay for health care expenses in retirement. Quite clearly this is an unattainable number for most workers—let alone low-wage workers—to save for their health care.[12]

Retiring into Low Wages

The retired restaurant workers we met thus far have illustrated the challenges of retiring on low-wage workers' income without a partner who has additional income and savings or programs that can lower costs (such as housing rent reductions). Camilla, a 69-year-old white bartender, tells a slightly different story. Camilla, like many women, found herself in restaurant work after she and her husband divorced. She needed a part-time job to help supplement her child support and found a bartending job just a few blocks from her house. She started in 1987 and retired in May 2017. Over the three decades Camilla realized that she would need additional income to support herself and her children. So while bartending, she worked at a local army base; she started out as a typist and through her career advanced to management. However, Camilla continued to tend bar part time while working full time at the army base. In 2011 the army base closed down—and while she was able to collect her government pension, it wasn't enough. So she stayed behind the bar. Like Steven (Chapter 3), Camilla is a worker with a safety net from her middle-wage job, but that job was not enough to survive on during her working years (which led her into bartending) and when she retired from that work (which forced her to stay bartending even after her retirement from the federal government).

Now that the restaurant she worked at has closed, she is concerned about her future. "My town is reevaluating our homes. Our tax bill may go up and I am really worried about paying my secondary insurance that's $400 a month. And I still have my mortgage payments for a little while longer." Homeownership was not the solution to retirement. But this runs counter to the narrative of the American Dream—own your own home as a marker of success. So Camilla may be retired from the army but not the bar. In fact, two weeks after we met she started a new job bartending at a performing arts center. That job, however, is just temporary for the summer; come September she will be unemployed again. "Then what. . . . I don't know. Maybe move to Georgia or Florida where the cost of living is less. It's so hard to leave my friends and community, but that may be the only way to survive."

Camilla's story highlights a larger issue that has been a backdrop in all these stories: the challenges that low-wage workers face are not that different from those of middle-class workers. Several individuals in my focus groups in New Jersey and Massachusetts felt that they had been preparing for retirement, but when they faced the reality of retirement, they learned they were often ill-prepared. Many talked about having saved for retirement but quickly learned that they had not been able to save enough and found themselves outliving their savings. For instance, one union member lamented: "Working those years, saving, I thought I would be 100 percent secure. Instead, I feel like I've got zero!"

As a result, many retirees had to figure out how to patch together a sense of economic security. Like Camilla, one way that seniors tried to address their economic insecurity was working longer than they had anticipated. One retired woman had to keep working even after she received social security: "I wasn't old enough for Social Security yet, so I had to either take a job or live with my kids. I would rather work 24/7. And even when I started collecting, I had to keep my job. I had no choice." Many low-income and middle-income workers feel that the retirement strategy of working longer or indefinitely is their best plan, out of necessity. They try to keep income flowing and do their best not to tap into whatever savings they may have. Yet it may also be one of the least secure plans.

What Could the Future Hold?

The restaurant workers and retirees I met all voiced serious concerns about their economic security. However, they were all trying to make it work even with the decreased social safety net and ever-increasing costs of living. They were piecing together their economic security like a difficult puzzle, and not all the pieces were seamlessly fitting together. Some tried to work as long as they could, but age discrimination and health concerns made that difficult. Others depended on what was left of their own safety net to close gaps. Still others helped out and were helped out by family and kin networks. None of these were effective long-term solutions. Some of the seniors were more successful than others, but all knew that at any point, their own economic security puzzle could be missing pieces or become unglued.

What did the retirees in New Jersey and Massachusetts think their future would hold? Many voiced concerns that benefits they had felt just years before were quite secure were instead today being depleted and might not be available to them in the years to come. One union member noted: "I belong to Amalgamated local and we had our own pension. I'm concerned that those investments will not be enough to cover the benefits promised, and there are not enough member contributions anymore with the decreasing number of union members and lack of growth in the stock market—so it's just what we already have in there." Another senior—also a union member—said, "We were very fortunate at UAW [United Automobile Workers] but now we're hurting—lost bonuses, big copays, lost benefits, dental; they have cut back on about a third of the money we thought we had due to the bankruptcy of General Motors. They are now looking to cut more—other companies are also doing this." But as concerned as the seniors were for their own futures, they were much more concerned about their children and grandchildren. Many seniors noted that their children were not able to save any money. One older woman said, "My son can't save anything. He's working seven days a week, and he has a wife and a daughter, and his wife went back to school because she lost her job. He is very upset about not being able to save; he told me I need to have life insurance."

Another senior alluded to the changing labor market and his concerns about his children's ability to be economically secure—and the challenge of trying to help his children while they are trying to help him. "It's just that nowadays, the way things are with the economy, young people are losing jobs or working part time. You have to help them get an education and get student loans. It's a back-and-forth; you're trying to help them and they're trying to help you."

Others said that current labor market structures are impacting their children's economic security. "This generation will have a harder time to survive than we did. When a company decides to eliminate their workforce, seniority doesn't count. My daughter is very stressed and can't leave a job she wants to leave. . . . I want to help her so she can change jobs." Some tried to emphasize to their children that they would need to save: "My security now is OK—I don't do too many extra things. I've learned to be content with whatever lot I'm in. . . . I have tried to teach my children about savings, but my daughter doesn't have a job."

And several seniors felt that the supports that they have now—social security and housing—would not be available for their children. They very much feared the further erosion of the social contract. "My concern is for the future and the kids. . . . For me, I look up at the sky and I'm OK. . . . I don't think the future will be good for the kids. . . . social security . . . that's a little scary. We got to explain to children that we can't lose social security or Medicare. It's an insurance program, not an entitlement; we need that."

Despite the challenges, many retirees expected to continue to make sacrifices in their basic needs in order to get by. Several of them harked back to an earlier time of their lives—the Great Depression of the 1930s—and lamented that they often felt they were back in a similar situation. At the same time, they worry about their children and grandchildren who have not been tested by such challenges. "Most of us here are from a generation of parents who were the tough generation; somehow we'll survive. I don't know about our kids, though; [when I was] a kid, my parents were just trying to survive, get food on the table. There was one pair of sneakers for me and my brothers to share, holes in our shoes. Things have gone backward. Our generation lived through the Depression in the early 1930s; we learned the need of being secure, of taking care, making sacrifices, buying things you can afford. Younger people haven't gone through that. We were able to take care of our families, send kids to college." And anxiety for the future is not just felt by retirees. A 2017 survey of the National Institute on Retirement Security found that Americans in general are quite anxious about their economic security in retirement: 80 percent felt that the average worker cannot save enough for their own retirement.[13] A clear majority does not think individual-level approaches to retirement savings is a sustainable way forward.

Yet despite their concerns, several people I met still held out hope. They spoke of hope in going forward; some hoped for a time to come when people knew that if they did the right things—worked hard and saved—there would be employer and/or government programs and policies to help them be more secure in their retirement. Others were hopeful that things would have to get better and that people would demand it. And a small number held out hope that their economic security was just a "blip" on the economic scene. They thought of themselves as the unfortunate group who retired at the start of the Great Recession. They had to believe that for those coming after them, there would be brighter days ahead.

Conclusion

Economic insecurity appears to pervade the retirement years of most of the seniors with whom I spoke. They highlighted the concerns they had for their own futures and that of their families. Those who had access to supports—particularly housing—were appreciative of how critical that support was to their economic security but also painfully aware that supports often did not close the economic security gap, nor were they in plentiful supply. Many seniors live in fear that the supports will be eliminated or reduced, thereby making an already precarious situation even worse. These are serious fears—nationally, we have seen cutbacks in many of the supports and services that seniors cited, and with large percentages of seniors living below the Elder Economic Security Standard Index for their family types, access to supports become even more critical.

The experiences of aging and inequality today raise several concerns for older workers in the future. Retirees today are struggling, yet many had access to some form of employment-based benefits and/or public supports. Many seniors—including some who had what were considered good jobs—struggled to cover health care and housing costs, and those with savings lived with the fear of those savings running out. The seniors who reported any semblance of economic security had a combination of retirement savings and social safety nets such as Medicare/ Medicaid and housing subsidies. However, those supports and personal savings were in short supply and in too many cases never closed the economic security gap. The retirees of tomorrow may not be that lucky. Older low-wage restaurant workers have challenges making ends meet today, and many are not able to save for their retirement. These workers are also coming into their later years at a time when public supports such as housing, food stamps, health insurance, and transportation are under attack. Many of the low-wage seniors stressed that the little they did receive from public subsidies made a significant difference in their economic lives. How then will those who are working on less be expected to age with dignity when they are no longer working?

Indeed, reflecting on the experiences of all the retirees we met in this chapter, their experiences not only shed light on economic challenges in retirement but also raise great concern regarding what will become of the generation of workers coming up the pike who are perhaps even less prepared for a time when they can no longer work. These older workers did the right thing—they worked but often did not have employment packages that offered them health care and retirement savings vehicles. Some had savings; some had savings wiped out by illnesses. Some had partners who had savings and health insurance that they could draw on. Some were depending on kin networks. They all were concerned about both if and when they would retire. And some felt they never would retire. Others knew their health would fail and like the retirees earlier were scared for that future. Some were trying new ways of retiring—embracing the growing gig economy or depending on networks of friends to share resources. Others tried to figure out ways out of low-wage work and were trying to make their college degrees work for them, sometimes over a decade since they earned them. And inequality also shaped these workers' lives and retirement plans. They faced gender and age discrimination as they attempted to work longer. Low wages and the devaluation of service work made paying their bills difficult and preparing for retirement quite daunting. Many who were promoted in restaurant work too often found that advancement in low-wage industries does not necessarily translate into economic security.

And while they all enjoyed work, their narrative was not about the desire to work well into retirement for pleasure, it was about the need to work for survival. Retirement was not in their framework economically, though they feared that physically they could not keep up the work. And some who thought they could one day retire disregarded the traditional paths—having a secure retirement savings as their safety net. Instead they often tried to think outside the box—sharing resources and living expenses with others or trying to "strike it rich" in the gig economy. Many fell back on the American Dream ideology, such as planning to become the entrepreneur who would start a business and reap success. Where these workers will be in twenty years is not known, but it is clear that their destinies are hanging in the balance.

CHAPTER 5

Crisis or Come Together

The retirement system carries with it a deep history of both perceived and real challenges. What frames many of these challenges is the dichotomy between the belief in a clear transition from retirement preparation and saving that is a socially shared value of defined benefit plans and support programs, versus one where the onus and risk of retirement falls on the individual worker. Woven throughout this book is clear evidence of how these economic changes have forced retirees and workers to redefine their own American Dream, often to one that means just getting by, and sometimes by making sacrifices along the way. They have altered what they see for their future and how they are prepare for it; many report that there will be no retirement for them. Further, retirement is intimately intertwined with the labor market, as one's labor market status often predicts one's ability to save for retirement. The stories of the restaurant workers show that for far too many, it is just impossible to retire. As a result, social inequalities in the labor market are amplified in retirement.

The earlier chapters demonstrate that the economic challenges threatening low-wage workers in the restaurant industry are not indicators of a future crisis—these are the challenges retirees face currently. The crisis is upon us, and as the baby boomers retire in force, it will only get worse, especially for those in low-wage work. Instead of Americans sailing on a rising tide of social security and support into retirement, too many seem to be on a sinking ship that stops short of the serene golden years they thought their hard work promised them. The retirement system is broken not just for low-wage workers but for middle-wage workers as well. And this is no secret—86 percent of Americans believe that our country is facing a retirement crisis.[1] And they are quite correct—the average retirement savings balance of an American between ages 40 and 55 is $14,500, and the median savings in an American 401(k) account is $18,433.[2] This is not just a crisis for the poorest Americans—it is a crisis for all Americans. So many Americans "did the right thing" but are now confronting a mounting catastrophe. Too many have banked on social ideals and structures that are not coming through for them.

What will retirement prospects be for the workers in their thirties and forties that we met? What will their lives look like when they think about their retirement in 2035? For many of them, there will be no retirement. They will need to continue working in order to live. For others who cannot work—because of age discrimination or illness—their future is even more uncertain. Without adequate income or savings, they have no path to retire and will age into extreme poverty. In the next thirty years, those with middle-class jobs will be dependent on their 401(k) plans, which can be easily negatively impacted by market forces and cause these workers to incur debt from their working years. Like the retirees of today, they too may find their incomes being stretched to the limit by higher medical costs or by the need to provide economic support to their family. As they attempt to reconcile those experiences in retirement, they will find their retirement years filled with economic insecurity.

However, today's low-wage and middle-wage workers do not have to be doomed to working and aging in economic insecurity. Changes can be made to improve workers' lives to ensure that they can age with security. In this final chapter I address ways our current labor market experiences cannot provide for a secure retirement, along with detailing a new social contract framed by progressive public policies, reenvisioned workplace practices, and new pathways to economic security in retirement for aging workers.

Key Findings

The workers and retirees discussed in this book constitute a group who, one would say, did the "right thing" and followed the advice of the

American Dream mythology by working hard their entire lives. Some thought they would be prepared for retirement, but instead far too many of them were struggling. Health care was often their biggest concern and largest expense. And if they did have savings, it never seemed like it would be enough—some struggled and made hard choices to make ends meet; others depended on family for support, and several saw some of their retirement income stretched to help adult children and grandchildren. Many saw their 401(k)s depleted by the economic recession and did not have the time to replenish their losses. As a result, some attempted to reenter the labor market to make ends meet but often faced varying forms of discrimination. Public supports clearly mattered to the retirees' economic survival, although all too often those supports were not enough to completely close the economic security gap. Finally, inequality shaped individuals' retirements. Whether it was the amplification of the gender pay gap in social security payments, the struggle to access affordable housing, or the age discrimination they experienced, too often inequities affected how or whether retirees were getting by.

One common thread is that the intersections of race, class, age, and gender impact retirement and work. Corey Abramson succinctly noted that "who lives to grow old in America and who dies before they have the chance is determined in large part by social inequalities that reflect persistent racial, socioeconomic and gender-based divisions that are central to social stratification in America. . . . Consequently some of the most powerful connections between inequality and old age play out before old age is ever reached."[3] Abramson's durable inequalities are evidenced in the stories of both the retirees and the older low-wage workers. This point is pivotal to hypothesize what retirement will be like for the older workers we met in the restaurant industry.

What is so unfortunate is that gender and racial discrimination in the working years is so intimately tied to the retirement situation. We saw that women who faced a gender wage gap at work saved less for retirement and contributed less to their social security. So often the choices workers may have made—consciously or more subtly—in the labor market, following their passion to enter food service or taking time out to care for their families, affected their economic security in old age. What is more concerning is that the Americans' income inequality during the current economic recovery is only poised to continue and amplify because of its impact on retirement savings. As retirement accounts are increasingly concentrated in the top income distribution, may middle-income and lower-income workers have saved far too little. As a result, the wealthy get to enjoy their retirement years, while middle-income and lower-income seniors struggle.

Yet this has not always been the case, nor is it destined to be our future. As Teresa Ghilarducci states, "There was once a broadly equal distribution of retirement time across divisions of class and race."[4] And as has been noted throughout this book, from the time of the New Deal the possibility of a secure retirement was democratized and a reality for many. In fact, as recently as the 1980s as a result of Social Security, Medicare, pension plans, and disability insurance, low-income and high-income Americans spent roughly the same number of years in a relatively comfortable retirement. These are the policies, along with other aspects of our social safety net, that are currently under assault.

So how might a better understanding of the experiences of some of the most vulnerable in our labor market and retirement worlds create the policies and workplace practices that ensure economic security for all workers and retirees? I suggest the need for a new social contract for the America worker—one that ensures security both while working and when one can no longer work. First, to have a secure retirement one first needs an economically secure work life. Hence, a central part of a new social contract is improving jobs so they offer wages that provide for economic security, benefit packages, and career ladders that offer real advancement. Second, we must, as several commenters say, "rescue retirement." Individuals must have a mixture of social safety net assistance and savings vehicles that can provide the income and security they need to retire with dignity. Finally, health care concerns were paramount for retirees and workers; hence we must ensure that affordable health care during one's working years and retirement years is available and financially viable. I address each of these three tenets of a new social contract in the following sections; these tenets can be translated into policies that can help reduce inequality not only in one's working years but also in retirement.

I. Improving Jobs

Quite simply, if we are a country dependent on individuals saving for retirement, workers need to be in jobs where this is a real likelihood. Jose, Don, Sonja, and Jim all saw that the key to their retirement and that of their colleagues was policies that improved their jobs. Thus they saw working toward those policies as part of their retirement strategy. Only 20 percent of restaurant work offers the economic security needed to survive. As a nation we need to commit to increasing that to 100 percent so that all workers, regardless of job, have an opportunity for security. While there are still many middle-skill and middle-wage jobs in our economy, most workers are not in those jobs,[5] as these jobs represent a decreasing share of the American labor market. In their stead, the economy is witnessing a significant increase in the share of low-wage work. We need to be committed—through public policy and workplace practices—to improve these growing jobs so that workers can live and retire with security.

Next, we need to make a concerted effort to improve our low-wage jobs by ensuring collaboration between private sector changes and public sector supports. For example, we need to encourage high-road management practices—practices that engage front-line workers in problem solving and decision making and provide them with the training and skills to do this well—to improve the quality of service jobs and the quality of services provided. For instance, not all service jobs are the same, even within the same broad occupational category. Researcher Annette Bernhardt noted that in retail work, "markets for high-income customers or products requiring expert advice, multi-skilled and better trained workers are required—they need to have the technical background to give advice, the soft skills to build relationships with customers, and the ability and knowledge to make decisions on their own."[6] For example, she states that Home Depot workers earn significantly more than other retail workers, are typically employed full time with benefits, and have significantly less job turnover. Moreover, since Home Depot employs a decentralized management, departments within the store are run autonomously and hourly sales associates have considerable power to solve customers' problems and resolve customer complaints. In contrast, service jobs at mass discounters or fast-food restaurants are characterized by part-time work at low wages, along with increased levels of routinization and management control.

While higher-quality service jobs are not the norm, lessons from studies of management practices and work organization can be integral to the restructuring of service jobs in the future. Additionally, it is necessary to unpack not only the nature of work organization but also the characteristics of workers. Even within the same occupations, lower-status service jobs are predominantly filled by lower-educated, minority, immigrant, and female workers. As the service economy grows, it can continue to bifurcate, with better jobs going to higher-status workers. Tied to this is the need to direct firms away from low-cost, low-skills strategies to higher-value product markets where higher skills are needed.[7]

Comparative analysis can be important in not only identifying high-road management practices but also understanding the role of national labor market institutions in improving service jobs. Economists Eileen Appelbaum and John Schmitt found significant differences in low-wage work in high-income countries. Specifically, when unions retain much of their traditional strength and influence, where employment regulations provide workers with protections against layoffs, or where a national minimum wage provides an effective floor that enables most workers to rise above the low-wage threshold, employers are less able to evade institutional constraints on their ability to lower wages and reduce employment security.[8]

In addition to high-road management, workers need benefits and supports to move toward economic security. Public policy is critical here. However, whether workers and their families have access to health care, paid leave, flexible scheduling, and living wages are largely decisions left to employers. The absence of comprehensive social insurance or govern-mental protections results in a vastly unequal labor market, in which workers who fill low-wage jobs face many compounding issues. For in-stance, little national legislation is directed toward improving the ways workers can better address work and family demands. The Family and Medical Leave Act (FMLA), which provides workers with a statutory right to up to twelve weeks of job-protected unpaid leave, is limited in its scope, covering only workers who meet certain requirements (e.g., those who work at large companies and have specific care requirements). Many low-wage workers do not meet the criteria, and even if they do, they cannot afford to take unpaid leave. Companies that have fewer than fifty employees (about 28 percent of companies in the United States) are not required to comply with the FMLA. Too many workers are forced to work sick because they do not have access to paid sick days. This not only is a health concern for all of us who come in contact with these workers (or the food they may be serving us) but also tends to exacerbate illnesses of workers, causing long-term health impacts. One way to improve jobs is to provide federally mandated paid family leave and sick days.

And as evidenced throughout this book, the minimum wage is cur-rently not enough for families to meet their day-to-day expenses, let alone save for retirement. Therefore the minimum wage must be replaced with economic-security wages. Importantly, not all low-wage workers are even earning the minimum wage—restaurant workers, as one example, are often paid the subminimum wage and must rely on tips. Thus, the subminimum tipped wage must be eliminated at the federal level; work-ers should not depend on the whims of customers for their income, which also goes unreported. And without significant policy reform that ensures that workers and their families have some level of basic economic security, it is necessary to create pathways to the upper end of the labor market where these labor market rewards are more plentiful.

Workers are forced to carry the burden of inequities they experi-ence while working into retirement. According the National Women's Law Center, a woman who works full time for forty years loses over $430,000 in lifetime income.[9] This lost income translates directly to lower retirement income, as women's savings and social security benefits are automatically shortchanged. And while equal pay has been the law of the land since the Equal Pay Act in 1963, equal pay remains elusive. While having the law is important, we must have stronger enforcement of equal pay—across gender, race, and age—ensuring that workers are able to be paid fairly throughout their lives, which will help them increase their savings for retirement. In addition, policies that strengthen the Equal Pay Act will help address disparities. For instance, proposals to provide incentives for employers to follow the law, strengthen penalties for violations, and prohibit retaliation against workers asking about wage practices are a step forward in closing the gap.[10]

In addition, workplace discrimination—particularly age discrimination—must be eliminated through enforced policies and greater workplace education. Workers also need effective venues to address inequity (through either legal or workplace channels). This is critical as workers report that they need to work longer in order to economically survive. Policy that roots out workplace discrimination in all its forms will allow individuals to continue to work as long as they choose. Moreover, lost income in the years leading up to retirement reduces the credits used to calculate a worker's benefits and may force workers to collect benefits early or tap any savings they have; both practices reduce lifetime benefits. While current laws outlaw age discrimination, they need to be strengthened. For instance, the Age Discrimination in Employment Act (ADEA) of 1967 must be updated so that the burden of proof is shifted back to the employer and not the plaintiff, keeping it in line with other civil rights laws. In fact, AARP has referred to the ADEA as "a second-class civil rights law."[11] In addition, advocates state that laws and policies need to address more subtle forms of discrimination, such as by prohibiting employers from using tactics that screen out older workers during the hiring process.

II. Securing Retirement: Social Security, Savings Plans, and Public Assistance
Throughout this book the workers who felt that they had some semblance of security were the same workers who had some safety net—

savings from a job outside the low-wage labor market, partners who worked in a job with employer-sponsored retirement savings plans and health insurance, and/or some type of social net (such as housing assistance). Yet many other workers are reaching retirement age without any of those nets. A central tenet of a new social contract is to ensure that retirement itself can be secure.

A. Social Security

In 2015 social security protected 26.5 million Americans from poverty, including 17.1 million retirees age 65 and older. It is the main source of income for half of all seniors and the only source of income for one third.[12] Social security is often the only guaranteed source of income for most of us. However, in their current state the benefits are not enough to provide an economically secure retirement. In fact, the average benefit for a worker is just over the federal poverty line for an individual.[13] Moreover, as of 2017, social security has $2.8 trillion in reserves. This means it can pay every benefit owed to eligible Americans for nineteen years, and then pay out three quarters of the benefit amounts after that time. Thus the modernization of the social security program needs to be addressed as part of a new social contract.

Recall earlier the Urban Institute study that found that one way low-income seniors could have greater security in retirement was to work longer. And the way that social security is structured, the longer a worker delays claiming benefits, the greater those benefits will be. Under the current structure, individuals can claim benefits at any age between 62 and 70. In order to maintain fairness, benefits claimed before age 70 are actuarially reduced so that the lifetime benefits are roughly equal for both early and late claimers.[14] And the difference is quite significant—benefits collected starting at age 70 will be 76 percent higher than those for retirees who started collecting them at age 62. Not surprisingly, then, to protect retirees, some legislators have attempted to raise the social security eligibility age.

However, like the stories of the retirees and older workers in this book, while one may plan to work longer it is not always the reality.

Age discrimination and health problems, for example, may make working longer difficult and sometimes impossible. One study found that one third of Americans reported they were unable to work past age 62 because their jobs were too physically demanding or because they could not find work at their advanced age.[15] Indeed, working longer and raising the social security retirement age as a strategy to reduce poverty in retirement will benefit higher-income workers and could be detrimental to lower-income workers. Therefore, just working longer to have greater social security benefits is not a sustainable solution for everyone and can reproduce income inequality in retirement.

The program itself needs to be more broadly modernized so that one is not forced to work indefinitely. There needs to be increased money in the social security fund. The Center on Budget and Policy Priorities (CBPP), along with others, suggests that increasing payroll taxes can help improve the program's solvency. They recommend increasing or eliminating social security's cap on taxable wages. In 2017 the cap was at $127,200 a year; raising the tax cap could close roughly a quarter to nine tenths of the gap and was supported by presidential candidates Bernie Sanders and Hillary Clinton. In addition, CBPP recommends expanding the type of compensation subject to social security payroll taxes, such as employer-sponsored health insurance and flexible spending accounts,[16] as increasing payroll tax rates would help the solvency. Increasing payroll taxes by 2.88 percentage points (1.44 percentage points for employers and employees) could maintain solvency until 2088.[17] A true social contract for workers would ensure that social security—the bedrock of retirement income—remains solvent for decades to come without a benefit reduction for any worker.

In addition, social security needs to be modernized to meet the needs of today's workers and retirees. Christian Weller and his colleagues at the Center for American Progress suggest ways to modernize social security to address the gender bias that emerges when women take time out of the labor market to care for family. They suggest a comprehensive plan that includes provisions to address poverty in aging by creating a minimum benefit level so that no American lives in poverty upon retirement, and raising benefits by 5 percent for Americans age 85 and older. In addition, they suggest improving survivorship benefits so that surviving spouses do not face large benefit cuts, and strengthening divorce benefits so that divorced people are eligible for more benefits. These changes will help lower-income spouses (typically women) stay out of poverty. In addition, they suggest creating a caregiving credit so that workers can temporarily care for ailing family members—something that negatively impacts social security benefits. And to help address economic insecurity among LGBT families, they suggest expanding spousal benefits to married same-sex couples. To pay for these changes they recommend gradually phasing in progressive changes to the benefit formula, eliminating the cap on the employer share of the payroll tax to increase contributions, treating cafeteria benefit plans like 401(k) plans for purposes of calculating the employer share of the social security payroll tax, using a more accurate inflation measure to achieve savings in the system, and allowing social security to invest some trust fund assets in the stock market to boost returns.[18] These proposals would help modernize social security so that it reflects the changing economic and demographic composition of our country and also addresses the economic insecurity gap facing so many retirees.

Further, many low-wage workers said that working off the books undermined their social security income. What may appear to be a short-term gain of nontaxed income is a significant long-term liability. The lost work credits for the years of under-the-table work negatively impacts one's income. One critical way to address this issue is increased worker education on the long-term and short-term consequences of unreported income, along with increased enforcement and penalties to employers for engaging in this practice. With economic insecurity so rampant, leaving any amount of income on the table is risky.

B. Retirement Savings

With a more modernized social security system, the question remains: How much individual savings do workers need to supplement social security, and how can workers amass those savings when they struggle to meet basic life needs? One significant change evidenced over the past decades has been the movement away from defined pension plans to defined contribution plans. These plans often do not provide a secure retirement and instead leave workers subjected to the financial markets' risks and fees. As the retirees with defined contribution plans experienced, the Great Recession left workers with less money saved than they contributed. Further, low wages and wage stagnation have made it difficult for workers to put savings into the defined contribution plans, leaving many workers ill-prepared for income after retirement.

This shift to the defined contribution plan, interestingly, was not meant to be a permanent solution to the retirement crisis, and a new social contract must acknowledge this reality. Ted Benna—the father of the 401(k)—has gone on record over the past few years to express his concerns about what the 401(k) has become. "The tool was never meant to serve as the main means by which workers save for retirement, but that is precisely what it became—increasing financial risk for workers along the way."[19] Benna's plan was meant to supplement income in retirement. The 401(k) account came into being as a clause in the Revenue Act of 1978. The clause said employees could choose to defer some compensation until retirement, and they would not be taxed until that time. Anthony Webb, a research economist at the Center for Retirement Research, noted that "401(k)s were never designed as the nation's primary retirement system. They came to be that as a historical accident."[20] While the notion that a central savings vehicle of our current retirement system came about because of an historical accident may seem absurd, it is our current savings reality. As such, this practice needs to be addressed. The stories from retirees and older workers indicate the risks involved in a system dependent on the 401(k) and the significant number of workers who have no access to any retirement plan.

Workers need savings vehicles other than 401(k)s, and some proposals for what these plans might look like have been developed. New School for Social Research economist Teresa Ghilarducci and Blackstone president Tony James propose to create Guaranteed Retirement Accounts (GRAs). The proposal would require employees and employers to each contribute 1.5 percent of a worker's salary to an individually owned GRA, and the savings would be managed by professional portfolio managers. Unlike 401(k)s, the GRAs would prohibit early withdrawals. This would help ensure that savings could be put into long-term investments and earn higher rates of return than short-term 401(k) investments. Another distinction from the 401(k) plan, is that retirement savings would not be paid out at once. Ghilarducci and James are concerned that providing a lump sum is a potential challenge to retirement security, as it leaves it up to retirees to determine how much money they should be using each year. In contrast, under GRAs, when workers retire, their savings are paid out in an annuity—a guaranteed monthly payment for the rest of their lives—eliminating the need to budget correctly or the possibility of outliving their retirement funds.[21]

State-based retirement plans could provide access to retirement savings accounts for millions of workers who do not have access to any workplace savings opportunities. Currently eight states have passed legislation to establish retirement savings programs for private-sector workers whose employers do not offer a plan, and several others have legislation pending.[22] Central to these plans is automatic enrollment and simplified savings program. In a traditional retirement saving plan, workers are not enrolled unless they specifically sign up. However, in automatic enrollment plans, workers are automatically enrolled unless they opt out.[23] This helps to address workers' tendency not to save, since they are automatically enrolled. For instance, under an automatic IRA, employers would automatically enroll workers into a payroll-deduction IRA. Employees would have complete control and could choose to opt out, change the default amount, and choose their investment option. Their contributions would be placed into one of only a few investment options, with those who do not choose otherwise contributing to a target date fund or similar investment.[24] An example of state-sponsored retirement plans is California's Secure Choice Program, signed into law by Governor Jerry Brown in 2016. Under this law, all businesses with at least five employees will be required to participate in the state retirement program if they do not already offer a similar retirement plan for their workers. Workers will be enrolled automatically but will be able to opt out at any time. If they remain in the program, 3 percent of their pay will be automatically contributed to the retirement account, but workers will also be able to change how much they save.[25]

Workers need access to savings programs, but for those programs to be most effective for lower-wage workers, many economists believe that corresponding tax code changes are needed. Weller notes that currently, tax deductions hold a greater value for people with a high marginal tax rate than for people with a lower marginal tax rate. He suggests that the tax system needs to be modernized to address the savings needs of lower-wage workers. He notes that the Retirement Savings Contributions Saver's Credit, commonly referred to as the Saver's Credit, was enacted in 2002 as a temporary provision and became permanent in 2006. The Saver's Credit provides individuals who make less than $30,750 a year and save for retirement up to a $1,000 credit on their federal income taxes, and provides a married couple who make less than $61,500 a year with up to a $2,000 credit on their taxes.[26] The Saver's Credit is structured like an employer matching contribution to an IRA. The credit rate is 50 percent for very low-income earners, 20 percent for filers with slightly higher incomes, and 10 percent for moderate-income earners. However, Weller observes that there is a low take-up rate for the Saver's Credit, because the credit is nonrefundable. Many low-income workers cannot receive the credit because they have little or no federal income tax liability. He proposes making the credit refundable and making more people eligible for the credit by raising the income limits, so that middle-income families can benefit. He notes that an income limit of about $70,000, for example, would reach approximately everybody in the 15 percent and 10 percent marginal federal income tax rate brackets and thus reach many families who currently do not qualify.[27] Weller and his colleagues at the Center for American Progress suggest an even more drastic tax change. They propose savings incentives by turning all existing deductions into one single tax credit—the Universal Savings Credit. With this credit, people would receive a flat percentage of their contributions to a predetermined savings account, regardless of their income and how much money they owe in federal income taxes.[28] Changes in the savings credit relative to the tax code could go a long way in helping lower-income families save more money and gain more of a benefit from the tax structure when they do so.

C. Public Assistance

Many of the provisions included in the previous sections—the modernization of social security and the creation of state-mandated savings programs—will be a great help to younger workers but offer little relief to many of the older restaurant workers we met. For workers who are just a decade or so from retirement, it is simply too late in their lives to save the amount of money they will need to retire. The same is true for struggling retirees—their ability to save is close to nonexistent at this point in their lives. Instead a successful retirement will not be grounded in their savings that they accumulate but instead by lowering the costs of their life expenses. We must provide access to affordable housing and health care in order to help bridge the economic security gap that seniors face. Recall the long waiting lists for affordable housing that the retirees reported. This often leaves seniors with limited options and certainly can result in homelessness.

Retirees also need enhanced supports for other life necessities. For instance, in 2015, 2.9 million households with seniors age 65 and older (8 percent) experienced food insecurity. Further, more than 1.2 million households composed of seniors living alone (9 percent) experienced food insecurity.[29] Access to the Supplemental Nutrition Assistance Program (SNAP) can help seniors better afford food and help bridge economic insecurity gaps. In addition, SNAP also helps improve health outcomes for seniors by addressing malnutrition and other maladies that arise from food insecurity. Other supports include ways to help subsidize electricity for seniors, along with an investment in a public transportation system that can minimize costs for travel to doctors or grocery stores. Through a renewed commitment to support programs, older low-wage workers can supplement their social security income and what savings they may have. However, in addition to this commitment, we need to ensure that these programs can close the gap.

Further, some of the new models that the restaurant workers were trying to develop can provide some direction for social policy. One theme that was clear from my interviews was that many older workers felt they needed to create their own infrastructure for retirement. Building on a shared economy, they want to form their own villages—shared housing, bartered services, and a network of friends. These shared communities can help address housing and health care needs, with people building their own support systems and pooling resources. Building on European models, everything from tiny house communities to "Golden Girls" living arrangements highlight the need for a social infrastructure as one ages.

And while these are innovative and may prove to be successful for many retirees, the premise is based on individual workers accepting retirement security as their own problem to solve. Even further, the model is predicated on the notion that a retiring worker has the social capital to populate that infrastructure. Sociologists use the phrase "social capital" to refer to the network of relationships between people. For several of the workers we met, the concept of turning their social capital into an infrastructure that can help support them seems on the surface a viable option. And in some cases—such as Anita's and Jill's stories—these social networks are evolving organically.

But this organically formed network—while offering cultural resources—also presents significant challenges. Abramson noted in his study of networks among senior citizens that these networks must inevitably deal with network shrinkage as members die. As networks shrank, not only were there emotional losses, but "the instrumental effects of losing a key person in the networks revealed and exacerbated their greater generable vulnerability."[30] Moreover, he found that inequality was embedded within these networks and stratified options and outcomes. Networks are embedded within broader contexts that can provide unequal access to resources. Abramson found that for seniors it was then not just "who you knew" but also what resources come along with their connections. And as these networks shrank, the effect across socioeconomic class was uneven. "Network shrinkage did not mitigate inequality leveling differences or hurting everyone similarly. Rather it highlighted differences."[31] Seniors from more affluent backgrounds simply had more resources to weather losses in their networks. Therefore, while new models of shared care and communities offer great promise, they cannot be expected to succeed for low-wage workers without larger supports and programs. Social programs and policy can be critical in mitigating this inequality. For instance, AARP suggests addressing Medicaid dollars as a potential funding stream. AARP researchers note that most Medicaid funding is dedicated to nursing homes and not community-based care. If we address this disparity, a greater number of older adults will have access to resources to age in place.[32] In addition, innovative programs that offer grants, tax incentives, or low-interest loans to collectives of individuals who are willing to form care communities that will support each other can help better distribute these opportunities.

III. Health Care

Concerns about health and health care weigh heavily on the minds of the greatest percentage of Americans. Many fear they are an illness away from economic despair. Medicare, which is run by the Centers for Medicare and Medicaid Services (CMS), is the nation's health insurance program for people age 65 and older and for those who are disabled. Created in 1965 when people over age 65 found it virtually impossible to get private health insurance coverage, it has made access to health care a universal right for Americans once they reach age 65. Since 2011, the year when first of the baby boomers reached age 65 and became eligible, the population of Medicare-eligible people has grown rapidly. By 2030, when the youngest boomers will have reached age 65, Medicare enrollment will nearly double to an estimated 80 million people.[33] And in 2010, the Affordable Care Act added a decade of economic security to the Medicare Trust Fund, increased free preventive services, and increased parity between traditional Medicare and private Medicare plans.[34]

However, even with Medicare, many older Americans face large out-of-pocket health care costs. Per the National Academy of Social Insurance, this occurs in three main ways. "First, most pay premiums for coverage under Part B and Part D of Medicare. Second, they may pay premiums to private Medigap plans or to Medicare Advantage plans to cover items not covered by traditional Medicare. Third, they must make direct payments to doctors, hospitals, and nursing homes for services not covered by their health insurance. Because the cost of health care has been rising much faster than both the general growth rate of the economy and the increase in Social Security benefits, if current trends continue, income after taxes and health care spending for the typical married couple will be no higher in 2030 than it was in 2000."[35] As a result, while Medicare helps seniors bridge some of the economic gaps, it is not enough. And many seniors are choosing between food and medicine, or managing their long-term health issues and paying their rent.

Despite its importance in helping seniors gain some economic security, Medicare is currently under attack. In 2017, with a Republican Congress and president, many advocates are quite concerned about the possible repeal of the Affordable Care Act[36] and the Medicare proposals put forth by Speaker of the House Paul Ryan. One of the first items House Republicans are proposing is to raise the eligibility age for Medicare from 65 to 67. In 2013, the Congressional Budget Office (CBO) analyzed the effects of raising the eligibility age to 67 and found that 5.5 million seniors would be affected and forced to find alternative sources of health coverage. The CBO estimated that 10 percent of these people—or 550,000—would become uninsured.[37]

As dire as those estimates are, with the current climate of possible repeal of the ACA, the effects of this would be far worse. "CBO's estimates assumed that under the higher eligibility age, low-income seniors younger than age 67 would have the option of finding coverage under Medicaid expansion if their states chose to expand Medicaid. The House Republican proposals to roll back Medicaid expansion and dramatically cut traditional Medicaid would take away this option for seniors in states that had expanded Medicaid, likely resulting in more of them becoming uninsured."[38] Changes in the Affordable Care Act and Medicaid along the lines of repealing without an adequate replacement and privatizing the Medicare system are dire for retirees and low-income workers. For instance, under the proposals to privatize Medicare, beneficiaries would not enroll in the current program; instead they would receive a capped voucher to purchase private health insurance or traditional Medicare. According to the National Committee to Preserve Social Security and Medicare, the voucher program would encourage insurance companies to manipulate their plans to attract the youngest and healthiest seniors. This would leave traditional Medicare with older and sicker beneficiaries whose higher health costs could lead to higher premiums that they may not be able to pay.[39] At the time of this writing the future of the Affordable Care Act and Medicare are in question. This creates a level of uncertainty for all workers and further amplifies the concerns for those who are close to a possible retirement.

Instead a new social contract must be premised on the notion that health care is a right, not a privilege, and that health care must be disaggregated from one's employment. In September 2017, Senator Bernie Sanders and several leading Democratic senators introduced Medicare for All to create a federally administered single-payer health care program, covering the entire health care continuum. Universal health care provides workers the opportunity to work in a job that they love, rather than searching for one that "comes with benefits." This helps to level the playing field for workers in jobs that are traditionally excluded from health care benefits. A universal health care program, such as what Senator Sanders has proposed, provides workers and retirees with the health care they need regardless of income or job. Particularly important is the need to eliminate copays and deductibles and cover long-term costs— all of which currently cost older Americans hundreds of thousands of dollars. The United States must follow the lead of other industrialized nations, which provide a universal public health care program for their citizens. Knowing that one has health care during their working and retirement years is central to economic security over the life course.

Final Thought

As current retirees know all too well, the path to economic security is complex and interconnected. Therefore we must commit to a new social contract that is just as robust. It cannot be implemented piecemeal but must be a comprehensive reform. None of the proposals regarding savings programs will help low-wage workers (young or old), as long as they are not even earning wages to cover their basic needs. They cannot save—mandated or not—if they do not have the extra income to save. As long as we do not address the structure and labor market rewards associated with low-wage work, workers will always choose survival in the present over saving for their future. We cannot address social security, health care, and retirement savings without addressing low-wage work. Conversely, those who do not have the basic right of healthcare will not be able to economically survive. Instead, whatever savings they have amassed is almost guaranteed to be wiped out when a serious illness occurs. Of course, I am not suggesting that any of these proposals is a "silver bullet" to magically avert the crisis. These ideas have been and continue to be floated and rejected. But we need to acknowledge that by not embracing them, we have already caused many Americans to suffer and have set ourselves on a path toward catastrophe.

We are on the verge of an economic catastrophe—many of today's retirees are struggling to get by, and tomorrow's retirees are facing even greater struggles. However, this catastrophe is not inevitable. While the lived experiences of retirees and older low-wage workers represent real concern, they also provide significant insights into what policies and programs can help them reach economic security. We need to have both the political will and social responsibly to safeguard retirement security for all workers. This is one attempt to get us there.

Methodological Appendix

In many ways this book has been a long time in the making. I harked back to some of my earlier ethnographic research and began to see that work with fresh eyes. In those earlier days, I was so focused on understanding the labor process and workforce polices in low-wage work in America that I did not ask the question "What happens after work?" What happens when our most vulnerable workers can no longer work? And how do inequities in the labor market translate to a postwork life? This book is a response to these questions.

It was in my early days of waiting tables during college and graduate school that my sociological interest in low-wage work took its roots. I observed my co-workers struggling in several ways—some of those struggles I shared with them, others I did not. One experience that I shared with other restaurant servers was how the tipping structure shaped the work, and in particular the emotional labor we were expected to perform. There was also the day that I earned my first VOID paycheck. This, I came to learn, was when workers earned so little each hour that once taxes were taken out of their pay, no money was left in the paycheck. Tipping was then my source of income, and as a result I became quite interested in learning more about it. Using the tipping process as a vantage point, I noticed that restaurant work epitomizes many of the characteristics of service work associated with emotional labor. At the time I was waiting tables I was also reading Arlie Russell Hochschild's now-classic 1983 work on flight attendants, *The Managed Heart*.[1] Similar to flight attendants, restaurant servers have to both *deliver* friendly service and *feel* happy as they serve each customer. However, distinct from the flight attendants' situation, servers' incomes can be negatively impacted if they do not feel and express the emotional requirements of service work. One's economic success is then predicated on being able to control the service interaction and receive a tip.

Yet despite the potential economic loss, I saw that servers do not simply adopt the emotional prescriptions of service work. In my first large ethnographic study of restaurant servers, *Juggling Food and Feelings: Emotional Balance in the Workplace*,[2] I found that while servers knew the emotional requirements, they did not always follow them. Using a framework of emotional balance, I explored how restaurant servers dealt with emotionally disconcerting work experiences. Specifically, servers go about their work with a sense of emotional balance—the felt experiences that accompany waiting tables—that is often taken for granted. As servers work, they confront disturbances (such as rude customers or not being tipped for their work) that throw off their emotional balance, as emotions force themselves into consciousness and become objects of attention, reflection, and action. Not surprisingly, most of the official scripts to restore emotional balance encourage the server to invoke a company-approved emotive state—the "service with a smile." However, in restaurant interactions neither the practices to realize the company's desired emotional state nor the emotional state itself are often achieved. Instead, individuals engage in numerous practices to deal with their emotions in the workplace. Servers choose, disregard, alter, and create different scripts based on the unique characteristics of the microsocial context.

In *Juggling Food and Feelings*, my findings were focused on how restaurant workers emotionally deal with bad tips and rude customers and how they create and re-create their self-identity within the organizational constraints of the tipping process. I wove the sociological theories of William James, Erving Goffman, Karl Marx, Anthony Giddens, and Arlie Hochschild into my analysis to understand how restaurant workers dealt with emotionally disconcerting situations—the starting point being my own observations and experiences in the field. This was my first foray into ethnographic research, but there was a gap in that book.

I have been exploring this gap for almost twenty years—how the emotional insecurity of the tipping process is connected to the economic insecurity in restaurant work, and by extension other low-wage jobs. What are the experiences of low-wage workers and how do they attempt to get by on minimum and subminimum wages? I spent years interviewing single mothers as they tried to balance work, family, and education to build the resources that would allow them routes to some semblance of security.[3] I surveyed 100 restaurant workers after Hurricane Sandy to document how their economically precarious situations were further exacerbated by a natural disaster that left so many of them doubly displaced—having lost their homes and their jobs.[4] And most recently, in 2014, I went undercover in the unemployment system to document how those who had so little struggled to survive without income during the worst recession in recent times.[5]

I had some insights during my ethnographic research in the unemployment system as several of the workers I spoke with had exhausted their unemployment benefits, spending whatever savings they may have had. Their struggles were palatable. Then there was a group of workers I met in the process of writing *Not Just Getting By* that stuck with me—older workers. Older workers who had decades of work experience found that they had a difficult time in the recession. The unemployment rate for people age 55 and older increased sharply since the beginning of the recession in December 2007, with a record-high level of 7.2 percent in December 2009. While the unemployment rate among older workers is lower than that for their younger counterparts, older people who are unemployed actually spend more time searching for work than younger groups. In February 2010, workers age 55 and older had an average duration of joblessness of 35.5 weeks, compared with 23.3 weeks for those who were 16 to 24 years old and 30.3 weeks for those who were 25 to 54 years old. The longer duration of unemployment among older workers is also reflected in a higher proportion of the unemployed who have been jobless for extended periods of time. For example, nearly half (49.1 percent) of older jobseekers had been unemployed for 27 weeks or longer in 2010 (after the official recession ended) as compared with 28.5 percent of workers who were 16 to 24 years old and 41.3 percent of workers who were 25 to 54 years old.[6] Through my research in the unemployment centers, the stories of these struggling older workers gave me the greatest pause. They had spent their savings during the years when they should have been earning; what was to become of them and their families?

This question burned even more in my mind just a few years later when I conducted focus groups with seventy-seven retired workers in New Jersey and Massachusetts to document retirement security and insecurity while working at Wider Opportunities for Women (WOW) in Washington, D.C. Many of the seniors I spoke with were not low-wage workers during their working years. Some were union members who built bridges and tunnels; others were teachers and managers in business in both states. These retirees found themselves struggling—emotionally and economically—in retirement. If this group was struggling—those who had done the "right" thing during their working years—how would those who spent their working years struggling even begin to think about retirement, yet alone survive it? This is a gap I knew we needed to understand. While I was working at WOW, I led a qualitative research project that focused on elder economic security in states where seniors faced the largest income gaps in retirement. WOW researchers quantified the income needed to retire with economic security throughout the country and, with funding from the Henry and Marylin Taub Foundation, began to put faces to the numbers. As Robert Weiss argues, interviewing allows us to capture the individual experiences of everyday life that would otherwise be lost. "The celebrations and sorrows of people not in the news . . . leaves no records except in their memories. And, there are, of course, no observers of the internal events of thought and feeling except those to whom they occur."[7]

The purpose of the focus groups with New Jersey and Massachusetts retirees was to chronicle the lived experiences of older Americans "struggling to get by" in the current economic climate, thus illuminating individuals' challenges and the ways they made ends meet. Five focus groups engaged seventy-seven diverse seniors in lively exchanges about their current circumstances, how they have found themselves in those circumstances, and how they are "getting by." I stratified the focus groups so they would include representation from seniors in subsidized housing, along with seniors who were retired New Jersey union members. One focus group took place at the Jewish Federation Senior Housing facility in Paterson (Passaic County), and two focus groups took place at Teaneck Senior Housing in Teaneck (Bergen County); these focus groups engaged seniors in subsidized housing. Two focus groups engaged retirees from several unions representing auto, manufacturing, administrative, and service industries (Bergen County). One of these focus groups was held at the Bergen County Central Labor Council meeting, and a second was held at a United Automobile Workers (UAW) retiree meeting. I now had a tome of data from which to draw from.

The stories of retirement insecurity of New Jersey and Massachusetts seniors, particularly those who had those "good jobs," got me thinking back to the restaurant workers I had worked with years before. If those who had more opportunities for a secure retirement were struggling, how would those who barely got by during their working years get by?. To understand how workers from lower-wage jobs manage their retirement, I spent several years interviewing (and in some cases shadowing) restaurant workers throughout the country. I began collecting interview data for this project while working at WOW, building on the national partners the organization had, such as Restaurant Opportunities Centers United (ROC United), along with my own restaurant networks. I got leads from my contact at ROC United, Teófilo Reyes, and then reached out to the possible interviewees to determine their interest in participating in the interview. In other cases I would reach out to some of the interviewees from my recent research on restaurant workers after Hurricane Sandy to ascertain their interest in participating in the study. And I used snowball sampling to further expand my pool. Once interviewees agreed, I would work with them to find a convenient place and time for the interview. Each interview lasted several hours, digging deep into the stories of their lives—how they got to where they were, and what they were planning for their future. Over several years I conducted in-depth interviews with thirty-one restaurant workers in person, via Skype, and over the phone. Several of their stories make up Chapters 2, 3, and 4. Unlike my focus groups with retirees, these interviews were structured so that I fully understood their career trajectories, along with their plans and concerns for the future.

I always tried to keep the interaction as natural as possible. I typically began by explaining the project and by also sharing my own experiences working in restaurants. This helped to break the ice at the beginning of the interview as well as to increase the comfort level of our conversation. For the in-person interviews (which occurred mostly for the interviewees who lived in New Jersey or New York City), meetings were held in a variety of places—the respondents' homes or workplaces, ROC United offices, or local coffeehouses. For interviews outside New Jersey or New York City, Skype or a telephone proved useful. In these cases it was a bit harder to have more intimate and natural conversations; however, as the call (video and audio) went on, respondents began to be very comfortable sharing information. I often took copious notes during the interviews, not only to help me more easily transcribe them, but also to enable interviewees to review our discussion in the moment and clear up any errors. I also encouraged them to reach out to me if they had additional thoughts after our interview. Some did, and sent me follow-up thoughts. Follow-up discussions allowed me to gather more data and increase observations at worksites. Each of the stories in Chapters 2, 3, and 4 have been anonymized to protect the identity of the respondents. Each has a pseudonym used in the text, and any identifying information has been omitted or altered from the stories. When specific restaurant names or other identifiable details appear, the inclusion was approved by the informant.

By posing questions about the "transition" to a postwork world I was able to go beyond the statistics on economic insecurity, minimum wage, and retirement savings accounts to learn about the stories behind them. I hope that my methods did those stories justice.

Notes

Prologue

1. Jayaraman 2016.
2. For some restaurant occupations, low wages are often tied to those characterized as "tipped workers." These are servers and bartenders but also bussers, bar backs, and hostesses, among others. The federal minimum wage for tipped workers—known as the "tip credit" or "subminimum wage" system—is just $2.13 an hour, less than a third of the regular federal minimum of $7.25. This rate assumes that combined earnings including tips will ultimately make up the income difference to bring the hourly wage up to the minimum wage so that total pay will approximate that of other low-wage laborers. As so much research has shown, this is a flawed assumption.
3. Jayaraman 2014, 5.
4. Shierholz 2014.
5. Shierholz 2014.
6. Shierholz 2014.
7. Jayaraman 2014, 71.
8. Bendick, Eanni, and Jayaraman 2009.
9. Gatta 2011.
10. Gatta and Unrath 2012.
11. Erickson 2004, 80.
12. Erickson 2004, 80.
13. Gatta 2009; Gatta 2000.
14. Centers for Disease Control 1993.
15. Jayaraman 2014.
16. Borkowski and Monforton 2012.
17. Occupational Safety and Health Administration 2017.
18. Claussen 2011.
19. Lawrence and Turrentine 2008.
20. Jones 2013.
21. American Sleep Association 2017.

22. Zhang et al. 2014.
23. Shierholz 2014.
24. Restaurant Opportunities Centers United 2011.

Chapter 1

1. Board of Governors of the Federal Reserve 2016.
2. WOW was officially closed in 2016, and their Elder Economic Security program is currently housed at the National Council on Aging in Washington, D.C.
3. D. Cooper 2015.
4. Ghilarducci 2015a.
5. Coleman 2015.
6. Morrissey 2016b.
7. U.S. Department of Labor 2016.
8. Denice, and Laird 2016.
9. M. Cooper 2014, 38.
10. Coleman 2015, 4.
11. Government Accounting Office 2015.
12. Butrica and Toder 2008.
13. Gatta 2015.
14. M. Cooper 2014.
15. Handler and Hasenfeld 2007.
16. Glenn 1992.
17. Sherman 2006, 49–50.
18. Hartmann, English, and Hayes 2010. Construction saw a 23.3 percent decrease in employment; manufacturing and trade, transportation, and utilities industries experienced 16 percent and 7.6 percent declines, respectively. Another 18 percent of job losses were in administrative and waste services (in which about 60 percent of workers are male). Conversely, education and health services (in which 77 percent of workers are female) saw an increase of 4.5 percent employment, and public administration/government (in which 57 percent of workers are female) also experienced 0.6 percent growth. The job loss in predominantly male industries led many commentators to dub this recession the "Great Mancession."
19. Hartmann, English, and Hayes 2010, 36.
20. Heidi Hartmann, Ashley English, and Jeffrey Hayes (2010) found that women of color also fared poorly in the recession and beyond. During the recession, African American women's unemployment rate was 13.4 percent; Hispanic women had an unemployment rate of 11.3 percent, while the unemployment rate for white women was 7.2 percent. Educational attainment also was a key factor in unemployment, as women with less than a high school diploma experienced the highest unemployment rate of any group, averaging 9.5 percent unemployment in the last decade, compared with 7.8 percent unem-

ployment for men without a high school diploma and 2.6 percent unemployment for women and men with college degrees. And when we compare among women, the average gap between those with and without a high school diploma or more (4.6 percentage points) is much larger than the gap between men with and without a high school diploma or more (2.4 percentage points).

21. Wider Opportunities for Women 2012.
22. American Association of University Women 2009, 2.
23. Taylor et al. 2011.
24. Schmitt and Jones 2012.
25. Schmitt and Jones 2012.
26. D. Cooper 2015.
27. D. Cooper 2015.
28. Carr and Wiermers 2016.
29. Semuels 2016.
30. Carr and Wiermers 2016.
31. Morrissey 2016b.
32. Sabadish and Morrissey 2013.
33. Women's Institute for a Secure Retirement 2015.
34. The Elder Economic Security Standard (Elder Index) is a tool to define basic economic security by family type at the city, county, and state level for retired individuals. The Elder Index was developed by the Gerontology Institute at the University of Massachusetts and Wider Opportunities for Women. In this example, a retired senior would need to have a monthly income of $2,880 in order to have basic economic security in retirement.
35. Wells Fargo 2016.
36. Fidelity Investments 2014.
37. Meschede et al 2011, 1.
38. Meschede et al 2011.
39. Nari 2013.

Chapter 2

1. Northwestern Mutual 2015.
2. Northwestern Mutual 2015.
3. Emmons and Noeth 2014.
4. Allianz Life Insurance 2015.
5. Taylor and Goa 2014.
6. Drinking among restaurant workers has been documented by both researchers and practitioners (Bourdain 2000; Tutenges et al. 2013). Traditionally the "shift drink"—having a drink toward the end of one's shift—is common practice and may extend to throughout the shift. Further complicating the situation is the readily available alcohol, the custom of bar patrons purchasing drinks for workers as a "reward" for good service, and the fact that many

restaurants (particularly noncorporate restaurants) do not have a policy outlawing drinking in the workplace.

7. M. Cooper 2014.

8. *Front of the house* refers to customer-facing jobs such as server, bartender, and hostess; *back of the house* refers to jobs that are performed in the kitchen (such as cook or dishwasher).

9. Neumark, Burn, and Button 2015.

10. M. Cooper 2014, 22.

11. Yadoo 2017.

12. The digital gig economy means one is using an Internet platform (such as Uber or Craigslist) to find gig work.

13. Pew Research Centers 2016b.

14. Yadoo 2017.

15. Yadoo 2017.

16. Pew Research Centers 2016b.

17. Watt 2016, 23.

18. Steinbaum and Clemens 2015, 4.

19. Kroeger, Cooke, and Gould 2016.

Chapter 3

1. Zamudio 2016.

2. Harris and Giuffre 2015, 36.

3. Harris and Giuffre 2015, 37.

4. Quoted in Harris and Giuffre 2015, 37.

5. https://www.bls.gov/oes/current/oes351011.htm.

6. Tung, Lathrop, and Sonn 2015.

7. Nickson, Warhurst, and Dutton 2005.

8. Pettinger 2004, 468.

9. Casselman 2015.

10. Casselman 2015.

11. Mitnik and Zeinberg 2007.

12. Restaurant Opportunities Centers United 2015.

13. Silva 2013, 146.

14. See the Restaurant Opportunities Centers United website for more information on the campaign.

15. National Employment Law Project 2012.

16. Pew Research Centers 2016a.

17. Jayaraman 2016.

18. Jayaraman 2016, 35.

19. Litwin 2016.

20. Hyperwallet 2016.

21. Ben-Ishai 2015.

Chapter 4

1. Ortman, Velkoff, and Hogan 2014.
2. Wider Opportunities for Women 2013b.
3. Abramson 2015.
4. Weller 2006.
5. Heidkamp, Corre, and Van Horn 2010.
6. Rho 2010.
7. Wider Opportunities for Women 2013a.
8. M. Cooper 2014, 91.
9. COLA refers to the cost of living adjustment on social security.
10. WOW calculates rent for a one-bedroom apartment in Passaic County at $1,344, similar to this senior's assessment of the rental market.
11. Wider Opportunities for Women 2013b.
12. Employee Benefit Research Institute 2017.
13. Oakley and Kenneally 2017.

Chapter 5

1. James and Ghilarducci 2016.
2. James and Ghilarducci 2016.
3. Abramson 2015, 134–135.
4. Ghilarducci 2015b.
5. Holtzer and Lerman 2013.
6. Bernhardt 1999, 29.
7. Korczynski 2005.
8. Appelbaum and Schmitt 2009.
9. National Women's Law Center 2016.
10. These proposals are all included in the proposed Paycheck Fairness Act, which was first introduced in 1997 and reintroduced in Congress several times after.
11. Frank 2017.
12. Odum et al. 2016.
13. Odum et al. 2016.
14. Ellis, Munnell, and Eschtruth. 2014.
15. Ellis, Munnell, and Eschtruth 2014.
16. Romig 2016.
17. Ellis, Munnell, and Eschtruth 2014.
18. Weller 2010.
19. Porter 2017.
20. Holland 2015.
21. James and Ghilarducci 2016.
22. The Pensions Right Center has a database of state programs and leg-

islation: http://www.pensionrights.org/issues/legislation/state-based-retirement
-plans-private-sector.

23. John and Gale 2016.

24. John and Gale 2016.

25. Lobosco 2016.

26. Aspen Institute 2016.

27. Weller and Helburn 2009.

28. Weller and Unger 2013.

29. Coleman-Jensen et al. 2015.

30. Abramson 2015, 124.

31. Abramson 2015, 143.

32. M. Scott Ball 2014.

33. National Academy of Social Insurance 2017.

34. Stein 2015.

35. National Academy of Social Insurance 2017.

36. The Tax Cut and Jobs Act of 2017 repealed the individual mandate of
the Affordable Care Act.

37. Calsyn and Huelskoetter 2016.

38. Calsyn and Huelskoetter 2016.

39. National Committee to Preserve Social Security and Medicare 2017.

Methodological Appendix

1. Hochschild 1983.

2. Gatta 2000.

3. Gatta 2005.

4. Gatta and Unrath 2014.

5. Gatta 2014.

6. Sok 2010.

7. Weiss 1994, 2.

References

Abramson, Corey. 2015. *The End Game: How Inequality Shapes Our Final Years*. Cambridge, MA: Harvard University Press.

Allianz Life Insurance. 2015. "Generations Apart Study." https://www.allianzlife.com/retirement-and-planning-tools/generations-apart.

American Association of University Women. 2009. "Simple Truth Behind the Gender Pay Gap." http://www.aauw.org/learn/research/upload/SimpleTruthAboutPayGap.pdf.

American Sleep Association. 2017. "Shift Work Disorder." https://www.sleepassociation.org/patients-general-public/shift-work-disorder/.

Appelbaum, Eileen, and John Schmitt. 2009. "Low-Wage Work in High-Income Countries: Labor-Market Institutions and Business Strategy in the U.S. and Europe." *Human Relations* 62: 1907–1934.

Aspen Institute. 2016. "How States Can Utilize the Saver's Tax Credit to Boost Retirement Savings." https://assets.aspeninstitute.org/content/uploads/2016/06/Savers-Credit_v8_full.pdf.

Ben-Ishai, Liz. 2015. "Volatile Job Schedules and Access to Public Benefits." https://www.clasp.org/sites/default/files/public/resources-and-publications/publication-1/2015.09.16-Scheduling-Volatility-and-Benefits-FINAL.pdf

Bendick, Marc, Rekha Eanni, and Saru Jayaraman. 2009. "Race-Ethnic Employment Discrimination in Upscale Restaurants: Evidence from Paired Comparison Testing." *Social Science Journal* 39, no. 10: 895–911. http://bendickegan.com/pdf/SOCSCI821.pdf.

Bernhardt, Annette. 1999. "The Future of Low-Wage Jobs: Case Studies in the Retail Industry." IEE Working Paper no. 10. https://eric.ed.gov/?id=ED440260.

Board of Governors of the Federal Reserve. 2016. "Report on the Economic Well-Being of U.S. Households in 2015." https://www.federalreserve.gov/2015-report-economic-well-being-us-households-201605.pdf.

Borkowski, Liz, and Celeste Monforton. 2012. "The Year in US Occupational Health and Safety." http://hsrc.himmelfarb.gwu.edu/sphhs_enviro_facpubs/33/.

Bourdain, Anthony. 2000. *Kitchen Confidential: Adventures in the Culinary Underbelly.* New York: Bloomsbury.

Bureau of Labor Statistics. 2015. "Occupational Employment and Wages: 35-1011 Chefs and Head Cooks." https://www.bls.gov/oes/current/oes351011.htm.

Butrica, Barbara, and Eric Toder. 2008. "Are Low-Wage Workers Destined for Low Income at Retirement?" http://www.urban.org/research/publication/are-low-wage-workers-destined-low-income-retirement.

Calsyn, Maura, and Thomas Huelskoetter. 2016. "House GOP Proposals Would Make Health Coverage Less Secure for All Americans." https://www.americanprogress.org/issues/healthcare/reports/2016/08/01/141954/house-gop-proposals-would-make-health-coverage-less-secure-for-all-americans-2/.

Carr, Michael, and Emily Wiermers. 2016. "The Decline in Lifetime Earnings Mobility in the U.S.: Evidence from Survey-linked Administrative Data." http://equitablegrowth.org/equitablog/the-decline-in-lifetime-earnings-mobility-in-the-u-s-evidence-from-survey-linked-administrative-data/.

Casselman, Ben. 2015. "It's Getting Harder to Move Beyond a Minimum-Wage Job." http://fivethirtyeight.com/features/its-getting-harder-to-move-beyond-a-minimum-wage-job/.

Centers for Disease Control. 1993. "Occupational Burns Among Restaurant Workers—Colorado and Minnesota." https://www.cdc.gov/mmwr/preview/mmwrhtml/00021845.htm.

Claussen, Lauretta. 2011. "Disproportionately High: Study on Injuries Among Retail Workers Surprises Researchers." *Safety and Health Magazine*, January 21. http://www.safetyandhealthmagazine.com/articles/disproportionately-high-study-on-injuries-among-retail-workers-surprises-researchers-2.

Coleman, Joseph. 2015. *Unfinished Work: The Struggle to Build an Aging American Workforce.* New York: Oxford University Press.

Coleman-Jensen, Alisha, Matthew P. Rabbitt, Christian Gregory, and Anita Singh. 2015. "Household Food Security in the United States in 2015, Table 2. USDA ERS." https://www.ers.usda.gov/publications/pub-details/?pubid=79760.

Cooper, David. 2015. "Raising the Minimum Wage to $12 by 2020 Would Lift Wages for 35 Million American Workers." http://www.epi.org/publication/raising-the-minimum-wage-to-12-by-2020-would-lift-wages-for-35-million-american-workers/.

Cooper, Marianne. 2014. *Cut Adrift: Families in Insecure Times.* Chicago: University of Chicago Press.

Ellis, Charles, Alicia Munnell, and Andrew Eschtruth. 2014. *Falling Short: The Coming Retirement Crisis and What to Do About It.* New York: Oxford University Press.

Employee Benefit Research Institute. 2017. "Savings Medicare Beneficiaries Need for Health Expenses: Some Couples Could Need as Much as $350,000." *Notes* 38, no. 1. https://www.ebri.org/pdf/notespdf/EBRI _Notes_Hlth-Svgs.v38no1_31Jan17.pdf.

Emmons, William, and Bryan Noeth. 2014. "Despite Aggressive Deleveraging, Generation X Remains 'Generation Debt.'" https://www .stlouisfed.org/~/media/Files/PDFs/publications/pub_assets/pdf/itb/2014/ In_The_Balance_issue_9.pdf.

Erickson, Karla. 2004. "Bodies at Work: The Dance of Service in American Restaurants." *Space and Culture* 7, no. 1: 76–89.

Fidelity Investments. 2014. "Millennial Money Study." https://www.fidelity .com/bin-public/060_www_fidelity_com/documents/fidelity/millennial -money-study.pdf.

Frank, David. 2017. "Feds Must Do More to Fight Age Discrimination." AARP. http://www.aarp.org/politics-society/advocacy/info-2017/eeoc-fight -age-discrimination.html.

Gatta, Mary. 2000. *Juggling Food and Feelings: Emotional Balance in the Workplace.* Lanham, MD: Lexington Books.

Gatta, Mary. 2005. *Not Just Getting By: The New Era of Flexible Workforce Development.* Lanham, MD: Lexington Books.

Gatta, Mary. 2009. "Restaurant Servers, Tipping, and Resistance." *Qualitative Research in Accounting and Management* 6, no. 1/2: 70–82.

Gatta, Mary. 2011. "In the 'Blink' of an Eye—American High-End Small Retail Businesses and the Public Workforce System." In Irena Grugulis and Ödül Bozkurt (eds.), *Retail Work* (pp. 49–68). London: Palgrave.

Gatta, Mary. 2014. *All I Want Is A Job: Women Navigating the Public Workforce System.* Stanford, CA: Stanford University Press.

Gatta, Mary, and Matt Unrath. 2014. "Measuring Economic Security in the United States." Presentation at the Garden State Employment and Training Association Conference, Atlantic City, New Jersey.

Ghilarducci, Teresa. 2015a. "By 2050, There Could Be as Many as 25 Million Poor Elderly Americans." *The Atlantic*, December 30. http://www.theatlantic .com/business/archive/2015/12/elderly-poverty-america/422235/.

Ghilarducci, Teresa. 2015b. "Senior Class: America's Unequal Retirement." *American Prospect*, April 24. http://prospect.org/article/senior-class -americas-unequal-retirement.

Glenn, Evelyn Nakano. 1992. "From Servitude to Service Work: Historical Continuities in the Racial Division of Paid Reproduction Labor." *Signs* 18: 1–43.

Government Accounting Office. 2015. "Retirement Security: Most Households Approaching Retirement Have Low Savings." http://www.gao .gov/assets/680/670153.pdf.

Handler, Joel, and Yeheskel Hasenfeld. 2007. *Blame Welfare, Ignore Poverty and Inequality.* New York: Cambridge University Press.

Harris, Deborah, and Patti Giuffre. 2015. *Taking the Heat: Women Chefs and Gender Inequality in the Professional Kitchen.* New Brunswick, NJ: Rutgers University Press.

Hartmann, Heidi, Ashley English, and Jeffrey Hayes. 2010. "Women and Men's Employment and Unemployment in the Great Recession." IWPR Briefing Paper. http://www.iwpr.org/initiatives/unemployment-the-economy.

Heidkamp, Maria, Nicole Corre, and Carl Van Horn. 2010. "The New Unemployables: Older Job Seekers Struggle to Find Work During the Great Recession." http://www.bc.edu/research/agingandwork/archive_pubs/IB25.html.

Hochschild, Arlie. 1983. *The Managed Heart.* Berkeley: University of California Press.

Holland, Kelly. 2015. "For Millions, 401(k) Plans Have Fallen Short." http://www.cnbc.com/2015/03/20/l-it-the-401k-is-a-failure.html.

Holtzer, Harry, and Robert Lerman. 2013. "The Future of Middle Skill Jobs." http://www.brookings.edu/~/media/research/files/papers/2009/2/middle%20skill%20jobs%20holzer/02_middle_skill_jobs_holzer.pdf.

Hyperwallet. 2016. "Payday in America: What American Workers Want in 2016." https://www.hyperwallet.com/app/uploads/Hyperwallet-White paper-Payday-in-America.pdf

James, Tony, and Teresa Ghilarducci. 2016. *Rescuing Retirement: A Plan to Guarantee Retirement Security for All Americans.* Austin, TX: Disruption Books.

Jayaraman, Saru. 2014. *Behind the Kitchen Door.* New York: ILR Press.

Jayaraman, Saru. 2016. *Forked: A New Standard for American Dining.* New York: Oxford University Press.

John, David, and William Gale. 2016. "Policy Design and Management Issues for State Retirement Saving Plans." https://www.brookings.edu/wp-content/uploads/2016/07/johngale_primer_policybrief_03182016-2.pdf.

Jones, Jeffery. 2013. "In U.S., 40% Get Less Than Recommended Amount of Sleep." http://www.gallup.com/poll/166553/less-recommended-amount-sleep.aspx.

Korczynski, Marek. 2005. "Service Work and Skills: An Overview." *Human Resource Management Journal* 15, no. 2: 1–12.

Kroeger, Teresa, Tanyell Cooke, and Elise Gould. 2016. "The Class of 2016: The Labor Market Is Still Far From Ideal for Young Graduates." http://www.epi.org/publication/class-of-2016/.

Lawrence, Nancy, and Andrew Turrentine. 2008. "Examination of Noise Hazards for Employees in Bar Environments." *Journal of SH&E Research* 5, no. 3. http://www.asse.org/assets/1/7/winter08-feature04.pdf.

Litwin, Orwin. 2016. "Reimaging Retirement in the Gig Economy." https://www.rstreet.org/wp-content/uploads/2016/03/57.pdf.

Lobosco, Kate. 2016. "7 Million Californians Are Getting a StateRun Retirement Plan." http://money.cnn.com/2016/09/29/retirement/california-retirement-plan/.

Meschede, Tatjana, Laura Sullivan, and Thomas Shapiro. 2011. "The Crisis of Economic Insecurity for African American and Latino Seniors." http://www.demos.org/sites/default/files/publications/IASP%20Demos%20Senior%20of%20Color%20Brief%20September%202011.pdf.

Mitnik, Pablo, and Matthew Zeinberg. 2007. "From Bad to Good Jobs? An Analysis of the Prospects for Career Ladders in the Service Industries." http://www.cows.org/_data/documents/1184.pdf.

Morrissey, Monique. 2016a. "In Time for Christmas: A "Progressive" Social Security Plan Scrooge Would Love." http://www.epi.org/blog/a-social-security-plan-scrooge-would-love/

Morrissey, Monique. 2016b. "The State of American Retirement: How 401(k)s Have Failed Most American Workers." http://www.epi.org/publication/retirement-in-america/.

Nari, Rhee. 2013. "Race and Retirement Insecurity in the United States." http://www.nirsonline.org/storage/nirs/documents/Race%20and%20Retirement%20Insecurity/race_and_retirement_insecurity_final.pdf.

National Academy of Social Insurance. 2017. "The Future of Medicare." https://www.nasi.org/learn/medicare/future-medicare.

National Committee to Preserve Social Security and Medicare. 2017. "Legislative Agenda for 115th Congress, 2017–2018." http://www.ncpssm.org/Portals/0/pdf/legislative-agenda-2017.pdf.

National Employment Law Project. 2012. "The Low Wage Recovery and Growing Inequality." http://www.nelp.org/publication/4050/.

National Women's Law Center. 2016. "Wage Gap Costs Women More Than $430,000 over a Career, NWLC Analysis Shows." https://nwlc.org/press-releases/wage-gap-costs-women-more-than-430000-over-a-career-nwlc-analysis-shows/.

Neumark, David, Ian Burn, and Patrick Button. 2015. "Is It Harder for Older Workers to Find Jobs? New and Improved Evidence from a Field Experiment." http://www.nber.org/papers/w21669.pdf.

Nickson, Dennis, Chris Warhurst, and Eli Dutton, 2005. "The Importance of Attitude and Appearance in the Service Encounter in Retail and Hospitality." *Managing Service Quality* 15, no. 2: 195–208. https://pure.strath.ac.uk/portal/en/publications/the-importance-of-attitude-and

-appearance-in-the-service-encounter-in-retail-and-hospitality(cd77c4ab
-5933-45ad-81a1-8703aba0cb89).html.

Northwestern Mutual. 2015. "Planning and Progress Study." https://www
.northwesternmutual.com/about-us/studies/planning-and-progress-2015
-study.

Oakley, Diane, and Kelly Kenneally. 2017. "Retirement Security 2017: A
Roadmap for Policy Makers: Americans' Views of the Retirement Crisis
and Solutions." National Institute on Retirement Security. http://www
.nirsonline.org/storage/nirs/documents/2017%20Conference/2017
_opinion_nirs_final_web.pdf.

Occupational Safety and Health Administration. 2017. "Home Health Care."
https://www.osha.gov/SLTC/home_healthcare/index.html.

Odum, Jackie, Eliza Schultz, Rebecca Vallas, and Christian Weller. 2016.
"Toward a Dignified Retirement for All." https://www.americanprogress
.org/issues/poverty/reports/2016/11/15/292351/toward-a-dignified
-retirement-for-all/.

Ortman, Jennifer, Victoria A. Velkoff, and Howard Hogan. 2014. "An Aging
Nation: The Older Population in the United States." https://www.census
.gov/prod/2014pubs/p25-1140.pdf.

Pettinger, Lynne. 2004. "Brand Culture and Branded Workers: Service Work
and Aesthetic Labour in Fashion Retail." *Consumption, Markets and Culture*
7, no. 2: 165–184.

Pew Research Centers. 2016a. "America's Shrinking Middle Class: A Close
Look at Changes Within Metropolitan Areas." http://www.pewsocialtrends
.org/2016/05/11/americas-shrinking-middle-class-a-close-look-at-changes
-within-metropolitan-areas/.

Pew Research Centers. 2016b. "Gig Work, Online Selling and Home
Sharing." http://www.pewinternet.org/2016/11/17/gig-work-online-selling
-and-home-sharing/.

Porter, Steven. 2017. "Why 'Father of the 401(k)' Says He Regrets Pushing
the Retirement Plan." http://www.csmonitor.com/Business/2017/0104/
Why-Father-of-the-401-k-says-he-regrets-pushing-the-retirement-plan.

Restaurant Opportunities Centers United. 2011. "Behind the Kitchen Door:
A Multi-site Study of the Restaurant Industry." http://rocunited.org/2011
-behind-the-kitchen-door-multi-site-study/#sthash.o2S1BNZV.dpuf.

Restaurant Opportunities Centers United. 2015. "Racial and Gender
Occupational Segregation in the Restaurant Industry." http://rocunited
.org/wp2015b/wp-content/uploads/2015/10/RaceGender_Report_LR
.pdf.

Rho, Hye Jin. 2010. "Hard Work? Patterns in Physically Demanding Labor
Among Older Workers." http://cepr.net/documents/publications/older
-workers-2010-08.pdf.

Romig, Kathleen. 2016. "Increasing Payroll Taxes Would Strengthen Social Security." http://www.cbpp.org/research/social-security/increasing-payroll-taxes-would-strengthen-social-security.

Rosenfeld, Jake, Patrick Denice, and Jennifer Laird. 2016. "Union Decline Lowers Wages of Nonunion Workers: The Overlooked Reason Why Wages Are Stuck and Inequality Is Growing." http://www.epi.org/publication/union-decline-lowers-wages-of-nonunion-workers-the-overlooked-reason-why-wages-are-stuck-and-inequality-is-growing/.

Sabadish, Natalie, and Monique Morrissey. 2013. "Retirement Inequality Chartbook: How the 401(k) Revolution Created a Few Big Winners and Many Losers." http://www.epi.org/publication/retirement-inequality-chartbook/.

Schmitt, John, and Janelle Jones. 2012. "Where Have All the Good Jobs Gone?" http://cepr.net/documents/publications/good-jobs-2012-07.pdf.

Scott Ball, Monica. 2014. "Aging in Place: A Toolkit for Local Governments." https://www.aarp.org/content/dam/aarp/livable-communities/plan/planning/aging-in-place-a-toolkit-for-local-governments-aarp.pdf.

Semuels, Alena. 2016. "Poor at 20, Poor for Life." *The Atlantic.* https://www.theatlantic.com/business/archive/2016/07/social-mobility-america/491240/.

Sherman, Rachel. 2006. *Class Acts: Service and Inequality in Luxury Hotels.* Berkeley: University of California Press.

Shierholz, Heidi. 2014. "Low Wages and Few Benefits Mean Many Restaurant Workers Can't Make Ends Meet." http://www.epi.org/publication/restaurant-workers/.

Silva, Jennifer. 2013. *Coming Up Short: Working-Class Adulthood in an Age of Uncertainty.* New York: Oxford University Press.

Sok, Emily. 2010. "Record Unemployment Among Older Workers Does Not Keep Them out of the Job Market." http://www.bls.gov/opub/ils/summary_10_04/older_workers.htm.

Stein, Judith. 2015. "Medicare at 50: Then and Now." https://talkpoverty.org/2015/06/30/medicare-50/.

Steinbaum, Marshall, and Austin Clemens, 2015. "The Cruel Game of Musical Chairs in the U.S. Labor Market." http://equitablegrowth.org/research-analysis/cruel-game-musical-chairs-u-s-labor-market/.

Taylor, Paul, and George Goa, 2014. "Generation X: America's Neglected 'Middle Child.'" http://www.pewresearch.org/fact-tank/2014/06/05/generation-x-americas-neglected-middle-child/.

Taylor, Paul, Rakesh Kochhar, Daniel Dockterman, and Seth Motel. 2011. "In Two Years of Economic Recovery, Women Lost Jobs, Men Found Them." http://pewsocialtrends.org/files/2011/07/Employment-by-Gender_FINAL_7-6-11.pdf.

Tung, Irene, Yannet Lathrop, and Paul Sonn. 2015. "The Growing Movement for $15." http://www.nelp.org/content/uploads/Growing-Movement-for-15-Dollars.pdf.

Tutenges, Sabastien, Trine Bøgkjær, Maj Witte, and Morten Hesse. 2013. "Drunken Environments: A Survey of Bartenders Working in Pubs, Bars and Nightclubs." *International Journal of Environmental Research and Public Health* 10, no. 10: 4896–4906.

U.S. Department of Labor. 2016. "Union Members Summary." https://www.bls.gov/news.release/union2.nr0.htm.

Watt, Peter. 2016. "The Rise of the 'Dropout Entrepreneur': Dropping Out, 'Self-Reliance' and the American Myth of Entrepreneurial Success." *Culture and Organization* 22, no. 1: 20–43.

Weiss, Robert, 1994. *Learning from Strangers: The Art and Method of Qualitative Interview Studies.* New York: Simon and Schuster.

Weller, Christian. 2006. "Pushing the Limit." https://www.americanprogress.org/issues/economy/reports/2006/07/19/2090/pushing-the-limit/.

Weller, Christian. 2010. "Building It Up, Not Tearing It Down: A Progressive Approach to Strengthening Social Security." https://cdn.americanprogress.org/wp-content/uploads/issues/2010/12/pdf/social_security.pdf

Weller, Christian, and Amy Helburn. 2009. "Public Policy Options to Build Wealth for America's Middle Class." http://scholarworks.umass.edu/cgi/viewcontent.cgi?article=1178&context=peri_workingpapers.

Weller, Christian, and Sam Unger. 2013. "The Universal Savings Credit." https://cdn.americanprogress.org/wp-content/uploads/2013/07/UniversalSavingsCredit-report.pdf.

Wells Fargo. 2016. "2016 Wells Fargo Millennial Study." https://www08.wellsfargomedia.com/assets/pdf/commercial/retirement-employee-benefits/perspectives/2016-millennial-retirement-study.pdf.

Wider Opportunities for Women. 2012. "Women's Work in 2011." http://www.wowonline.org/documents/TOP50OccupationsWomen2011.pdf.

Wider Opportunities for Women. 2013a. "Living Below the Line: Economic Insecurity Among Massachusetts Elders." http://www.wowonline.org/wp-content/uploads/2013/05/Living-Below-the-Line-Economic-Insecurity-Among-Massachusetts-Elders-Report-WOW-MAOA-2014.pdf.

Wider Opportunities for Women. 2013b. "Living Below the Line: Economic Insecurity and Older Americans." http://www.wowonline.org/wp-content/uploads/2013/09/Living-Below-the-Line-Economic-Insecurity-and-Older-Americans-State-Rankings-Sept-2013.pdf.

Women's Institute for a Secure Retirement (WISER). 2015. "The Pay Gap's Connected to the Retirement Gap." https://www.wiserwomen.org/images/imagefiles/pay-gap-connected-to-the-retirement-gap-2015.pdf.

Yadoo, Jordan. 2017. "Six-Figure Earners Are a Growing Share of U.S. 'Gig' Workforce." *Bloomberg News.* https://www.bloomberg.com/news/articles/2017-06-13/six-figure-earners-form-a-growing-share-of-u-s-gig-workforce.

Zamudio, Maria Ines. 2016. "For Some Low Income Workers Retirement Is Only a Dream." http://bigstory.ap.org/article/f3cd4a23739448a39a4a518e34b7cb8e/some-low-income-workers-retirement-only-dream.

Zhang, Jing, Yan Zhu, Guanxia Zhan, Polina Fenik, Lori Panossian, Maxime M. Wang, Shayla Reid, David Lai, James G. Davis, Joseph A. Baur, and Sigrid Veasey. 2014. "Extended Wakefulness: Compromised Metabolics in and Degeneration of Locus Ceruleus Neurons." *Journal of Neuroscience* 34, no. 12: 4418–4431.

Index

Page numbers followed by f indicate material in figures.